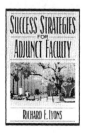  

Open-Book Testing: Why It Makes Sense

By Kay Burke, Ph.D.

Educators who allow students to take open-book tests are not teaching *for the test*; they are teaching *for understanding*. Most students agree that open-book tests are more challenging than traditional objective tests because they require high-order thinking skills rather than recall skills.

The greatest benefit from open-book testing may be that it encourages the type of thinking that will benefit students in the real world.

- Open-book tests focus on students learning important concepts rather than memorizing facts.

- They encourage students to utilize the lifelong learning skill of "accessing information" rather than memorizing data. In most jobs, people do not have to memorize formulas or discrete bits of data; they have to know how to find the important information they need in order to solve problems and complete projects.

- Open-book tests encourage students to highlight the text and organize their notes so they can find the information they need.

- Open-book tests encourage students to **apply** the information they have learned and **transfer** it to new situations, rather than just repeat the facts.

Sources:

Burke, K.B. *The mindful school: How to assess authentic learning*. Arlington Heights, IL. Skylight Professional Development.

Stiggins, R.J. (1985, October). *Improving assessment where it means the most: In the classroom*. Educational Leadership, pp. 69-74.

Wiggins, G. (1989, April). *Creating tests worth taking*. Educational Leadership, pp. 121-127

Wiggins, G., & McTighe, J. (1989). *Understanding by design*. Alexandria, VA: Association for Supervision and Curriculum Development.

THE IRIS CENTER
FOR FACULTY ENHANCEMENT
Peabody College at Vanderbilt University

WHAT'S IRIS?
The IRIS Center for Faculty Enhancement is based at Vanderbilt University's Peabody College and supported through a federal grant. The goal of the IRIS Center is to create course enhancement materials for college faculty who teach pre-service general education teachers, school administrators, school counselors and school nurses.

WHAT RESOURCES DOES IRIS HAVE?
IRIS course enhancement materials are designed to better prepare school personnel to provide an appropriate education to students with disabilities. To achieve this goal, IRIS has created free course enhancement materials for college faculty in the following areas:

• **Accommodations** • **Behavior** • **Collaboration** • **Disability** • **Diversity** • **Instruction**

These resources include online interactive modules, case study units, information briefs, student activities, an online dictionary, and a searchable directory of disability-related web sites. These resource materials are designed for use either as supplements to college classes (e.g., homework assignments) or as in-class activities.

STAR LEGACY MODULES
Challenge-based interactive lessons are provided using *STAR Legacy* modules. The following is a list of some of the many modules available on the IRIS website:
- A Clear View: Setting Up Your Classroom for Students with Visual Disabilities
- Who's in Charge? Developing a Comprehensive Behavior Management System
- You're in Charge! Developing A Comprehensive Behavior Management Plan
- Addressing the Revolving Door: How to Retain Your Special Education Teachers
- What Do You See? Perceptions of Disability
- Teachers at the Loom: Culturally and Linguistically Diverse Exceptional Students
- See Jane Read: Teaching Reading to Young Children of Varying Disabilities

CASE STUDIES
IRIS case studies include three levels of cases for a given topic, with each level requiring higher-level analysis and understanding from students.
- Fostering Student Accountability For Classroom Work
- Effective Room Arrangement
- Early Reading
- Norms and Expectations
- Encouraging Appropriate Behavior
- Reading: Word Identification/Fluency, Grades 3-5
- Reading: Comprehension/Vocabulary, Grades 3-5

WEB RESOURCE DIRECTORY
These online directories help faculty members and college students to search by category to find information about websites on the special education or disability topic of their interest.

All IRIS materials are available to faculty at no cost through the IRIS website http://iris.peabody.vanderbilt.edu or on CD by request to the IRIS Center (1-866-626-IRIS).

Instructor's Manual and Test Bank

for

Hallahan, Lloyd, Kauffman, Weiss, and Martinez

Learning Disabilities
Foundations, Characteristics, and Effective Teaching

Third Edition

prepared by

Candice Hollingsead
Andrews University

Bradley Sheppard
Andrews University

Boston   New York   San Francisco
Mexico City   Montreal   Toronto   London   Madrid   Munich   Paris
Hong Kong   Singapore   Tokyo   Cape Town   Sydney

ISBN 0-205-38874-4

Printed in the United States of America

10 9 8 7 6 5 4 3 2 1   09 08 07 06 05 04

Table of Contents

Chapter 1:   Basic Concepts   Pages 1–7

Chapter 2:   Causes of Learning Disabilities   Pages 8–14

Chapter 3:   Eligibility for Special Education Services   Pages 15–21

Chapter 4:   Parents and Family   Pages 22–27

Chapter 5:   Prevention and Intervention in Early Childhood   Pages 28–33

Chapter 6:   Transition Programming in Adolescence and Adulthood   Pages 34–41

Chapter 7:   Social, Emotional, and Behavioral Problems   Pages 42–48

Chapter 8:   Cognition, Metacognition, and Memory in Students with Learning Disabilities   Pages 49–54

Chapter 9:   Attention Deficit Hyperactive Disorder   Pages 55-59

Chapter 10:   Educational Approaches   Pages 60–66

Chapter 11:   Students who Experience Difficulties with Spoken Language   Pages 67–72

Chapter 12:   Students who Experience Difficulties with Reading   Pages 73–79

Chapter 13:   Students who Experience Difficulties with Writing   Pages 80–86

Chapter 14:   Students who Experience Difficulties with Mathematics   Pages 87–92

Chapter 15:   Participation in General Education Classrooms for Students with Learning Disabilities   Pages 93–98

CEC Content Standards Performance Rubrics for Chs 1 - 15   Pages 99-120

Introduction

This Instructor's Manual is a support to the textbook, *Learning Disabilities Foundations, Characteristics, and Effective Teaching* (3rd edition), by D.P. Hallahan, J.W. Lloyd, J.M. Kauffman, M.P. Weiss, and E.A. Martinez. It is provided as a complement to offer additional materials to the instructor. The manual contains the following chapter information:

> Chapter Outlines
>
> Chapter Questions
>
>> Multiple Choice
>> Matching
>> True and False
>> Short Answer
>> Essay
>
> Answers to Questions
>
>> Textbook Page Numbers
>
> Grading Guidelines
>
>> Textbook Page Numbers

Also included in this manual are **CEC Standards Performance Rubrics**, one for each chapter in the text, which supports the substantial standards-related material appearing throughout each of the text chapters. The rubrics appear together in one section of this manual, starting on p. 100.

The Chapter Outlines and Chapter Questions are arranged in reproducible fashion. The answers to each of the Chapter Questions can be found in the Answers to Questions and Grading Guidelines section along with textbook page number references for instructor use when students have questions about test items. The answers for the essay questions should be used as general guidelines. Suggestions have been given for essay specific responses, as well as general information that may be used to determine the acceptability of an answer. It will still be up to the instructor to decide exactly what will or will not be acceptable for a specific essay question. Additionally, point values may be reassigned on essay questions to reflect the importance an instructor wants to place on a particular topic.

Further support materials are available on the textbook web site: www.ablongman.com/hallahanLD3e. These include: Chapter Power Point Presentations, a Resources Section for additional readings, and Chapter Knowledge and Skills CEC Content/INTASC Standards Matrix.

Chapter 1: Basic Concepts

Chapter Outline

1. What Are Individuals with Learning Disabilities Like?

2. Why is it Important to Understand Learning Disabilities?
    1. Most Teachers Will Have Students with Learning Disabilities
    2. Understanding Learning Disabilities/Understanding Learning
    3. Many Students with Learning Disabilities Can Contribute Valuably to Society

3. Why Are Learning Disabilities Controversial?
    1. Difficulty in Defining Learning Disabilities
    2. Changing Definitions of Learning Disabilities
        1. Achievement Deficits
        2. Intra-individual Differences
        3. Psychological Processing Problems
        4. Neurological Deficits
        5. Exclusion
        6. Life-span Problems
        7. Social Relations Problems
        8. Co-morbidity
    3. Current Definition of Learning Disabilities
    4. Discrepancy between Ability and Achievement is Controversial
        1. Concept of Discrepancy
        2. Methods for Establishing a Discrepancy
        3. Consensus about Discrepancy
    5. Varying Criteria Used to Determine Eligibility for Special Education
        1. Responsiveness to Intervention
        2. Behavioral Consultation
        3. Standardized Protocol
    6. Eligibility in Practice
    7. Learning Disability as a Construct

4. How Many People Have Learning Disabilities?
    1. Demographics
        1. Ethnicity
        2. Gender
    2. Association with Other Disabilities

5. Who Works with People Who Have Learning Disabilities?

6. Can Learning Disabilities Be Overcome?
   1. Critical Need for Effective Teaching
   2. Life-Span Problems

Chapter 1: Basic Concepts

Chapter Questions

Matching

_____ 1. Learning disability may affect behavior in social situations and social problems may be a form of learning disability

_____ 2. A written agreement of educators and parents which delineates the student's education needs and the special education services that will be provided

_____ 3. The conflict between a person's potential for achievement based on intellectual ability and actual achievement

_____ 4. Learning disabilities may occur in combination with other conditions or individual attributes

_____ 5. The idea that learning disabilities continue into adulthood

A. Ability-Achievement Discrepancy
B. Comorbidity
C. Individualized Education Program
D. Life-span Problems
E. Social Relations Problems

True or False

6. More than 5% of school-aged children are identified as having learning disabilities.

7. The concept of learning disabilities as referring to below-average achievement that is not explained by other intellectual or sensory factors has yet to be widely accepted among educators and the general public.

8. Because learning disabilities are primarily apparent in educational settings, the role of educators is considered to be the most important professional roles in the field.

9. There is wide-growing support for the assumption that with proper intervention, learning disabilities can be reduced from a true developmental disability to a passing inconvenience.

10. Since learning disabilities are usually life-span problems, most adults who had learning disabilities as children continue to experience some problems later in life.

Multiple Choice

11. Which of the following statements about the use of accomplished people as examples of over-coming learning disabilities is most correct?
    A. A fair amount of assessment data has been collected to verify the disabilities of popular and historical figures.
    B. These examples can motivate students with learning disabilities to try harder and achieve more.
    C. Although motivating students is an important part of teaching, it is not the most important part of teaching students with learning disabilities.
    D. It has been relatively easy to identify historical figures and contemporary celebrities having a learning disability.

12. All of the following are identified components of Kirk's definition of learning disabilities *except*:
    A. below-average achievement or achievement-related behavior.
    B. psychological processing problems as either causal factors or at least correlated factors.
    C. cerebral dysfunction as a possible causal factor.
    D. inclusion of other disabling conditions and environmental conditions as causal factors.

13. Today's definition of learning disabilities:
    A. involves disorders of learning and cognition that are intrinsic to the individual.
    B. are specific in the sense that these disorders each affect a relatively narrow range of academic and performance outcomes.
    C. recognizes that they may occur in combination with other disabling conditions, but are not due primarily to other conditions such as mental retardation.
    D. All of the above.

14. When considering the demographics of learning disabilities which statement is most correct:
    A. The evidence of overrepresentation of certain ethnic/racial groups is not strong in learning disabilities.
    B. The number of boys and girls with learning disabilities is almost equal in the first through eighth grades.
    C. School psychologists are adequately trained to assess ethnically diverse students.
    D. Research has clearly indicated that boys tend to be identified as learning disabled due to bias, suggesting that their behaviors are more bothersome to teachers.

15. Researchers have been devising and refining instructional procedures that are more effective than earlier used strategies including all of the following *except:*
    A. cognitive training which includes exercises such as self-monitoring and self-instruction.
    B. direct instruction which includes the teacher explicitly detailing the information to be learned in large chunks.
    C. mnemonics which includes the use of key words and other ways of assisting memory.
    D. scaffolded instruction which includes gradual reduction of assistance and reciprocal teaching.

Essay

1. Identify and describe the historical theories of several major contributors in the field of learning disabilities.

2. Assess the relationship between these historical theories and the development of learning disabilities definitions over time.

3. Explain how the definitions of learning disabilities have influenced legal, ethical, and education policies and procedures.

4. Describe the issues of definition relative to personal society, family, culture, and label bias.

5. Explain your understanding of and respect for the heterogeneity of label characteristics in terms of development and lifelong effects.

Chapter 1: Basic Concepts

Answers To Questions

1.   E (p. 13)
2.   C (p. 7)
3.   A (p. 15)
4.   B (p. 13)
5.   D (p. 13)
6.   True (p. 5)
7.   False (p. 12)
8.   True (p. 37)
9.   False (p. 40)
10.   True (p. 40)
11.   C (p. 8)
12.   D (p. 13)
13.   D (p. 18)
14.   A (pp. 31-35)
15.   B (p. 39)

Essay Grading Guidelines

1.   Answers should include the profiles of different selected influential figures in the field of learning disabilities such as William M. Cruickshank, Samuel Orton, Katrina de Hirsch, Samuel Kirk, and Barbara Bateman. The responses should indicate the major contributions of each theorist to the field of learning disabilities. (pp. 10-11)

2.   Answers should include why the field of learning disabilities has been a controversial issue, how it has been difficult to provide a definition to learning disciplines, historical attempts to provide definitions, including Kirk's definitions and the major components of his definition that have been used by others, and the current use of the term. The answer should include the relationship of federal law to the definitions of learning disabilities. (pp. 8-18)

3.   Answers should identify the following laws: Education for All Handicapped Children Act (1975), Education of the Handicapped Act (1983), Education of the Handicapped Act (1986), Individuals with Disabilities Education Act (1990), Individuals with Disabilities Education Act (1992), IDEA Amendments (1997), and the pending Improving Education Results for Children with Disabilities Act (2004). After identify each of these acts answers should point out the main features of each act and then relate it to the emerging definitions as describe in number two above. (pp. 12-19)

4.   Answers should address the demographics such as the proportion of students with learning disabilities as compared to other disabilities, issues related to age, gender, ethnic make-up and socioeconomic status, the need to train school psychologists adequately, and guarding against bias. (pp. 28-38)

5.   While answers may vary since students are asked to demonstrate their knowledge of and respect for the issue, they should still indicate that learning disabilities are life-span problems and that there are no simple or easy cures. Answers should also point out that with proper instruction students with learning disabilities can learn most skills and subjects. Finally answers should show how learning disabilities continue into adulthood. (pp. 37-40)

Chapter 2: Causes of Learning Disabilities

Chapter Outline

7.   **What Causes Learning Disabilities?**
     1.   **Historical Context**
     2.   Reluctance to Accept Neurological Causes
         1.   **Problems of Inaccurate Measurement of Neurological Dysfunction**
         2.   **Emphasis on Behaviorism and Environmentalism**
     3.   **Toward an Acceptance of Neurological Causes**
         1.   Decrease in Popularity of Behaviorism and Environmentalism
         2.   Technological Advances in Neurological Research

8.   How Does the Brain Function?
     1.   **Neurons Send and Receive Messages**
         1.   **Neurons**
         2.   Soma
         3.   Dendrites
         4.   Axon
         5.   Terminal Buttons
         6.   Neurotransmitters
         7.   Synapse
         8.   Myelin Sheath
     2.   Different Parts of the Brain Have Different Functions
         1.   Brain Stem
         2.   Cerebellum
         3.   Cerebral Cortex
         4.   Frontal Lobes of the Cerebral Cortex
         5.   Parietal Lobes of the Cerebral Cortex
         6.   Occipital Lobes of the Cerebral Cortex
         7.   Temporal Lobes of the Cerebral Cortex
     3.   **Left and Right Hemispheres**
         1.   Broca's and Wernicke's Areas
         2.   Split-Brain Studies

9.   **How Can We Infer Neurological Dysfunction?**
     1.   **Postmortem Studies**
     2.   **Neuroimaging Studies**
         1.   MRIs
         2.   PET-scans
         3.   fMRIs
     3.   **Right-Hemisphere Brain Dysfunction**

10. **What Factors Contribute to Neurological Dysfunction?**
    1. **Hereditary Factors**
        1. Familiality
        2. Heritability
        3. Molecular Genetics
    2. Teratogenic Factors
    3. **Medical Factors**
        1. Premature Birth
        2. Diabetes
        3. Meningitis
        4. Cardiac Arrest
        5. Pediatric AIDS

11. What should Educators Keep in Mind Regarding Causes?
    1. Keep the Significance of Causal Factors in Its Proper Perspective
    2. Stay Abreast of Research on Causal Factors of Learning Disabilities

Chapter 2: Causes of Learning Disabilities

Chapter Questions

Matching

_____ 1.   Severe reading impairment that is thought to be due to neurological factors

_____ 2.   Results in problems in speech production and/or comprehension due to a brain injury

_____ 3.   Manifested in problems in math, self-regulation, and social functioning

_____ 4.   The ability to blend sounds, segment the sounds of words, rhyme, and in other ways manipulate the sounds of spoken words

_____ 5.   Cause of a disability or an abnormal condition

A.   Aphasia
B.   Dyslexia
C.   Etiology
D.   Nonverbal Learning Disabilities
E.   Phonological Awareness

True or False

6.   One reason for a presumption of neurological dysfunction in learning disabilities is that there is often no other plausible explanation for the child's failure to learn.

7.   Executive functions - the ability to regulate one's behavior through working memory, inner speech, control of emotions and arousal levels - takes place in the cerebral cortex.

8.   In the perceptual realm, students with nonverbal learning disabilities have difficulties with visual-spatial and tactual tasks, but do not exhibit the same difficulties in math, self-regulation, and organization.

9.   Recent studies suggest that reading disability is a familial condition.

10.   Researchers have consistently found a greater degree of reading disabilities and speech and language disorders in monozygotic twins than in dizygotic twins.

Multiple Choice

11. There was an early hesitancy for researchers and practitioners to accept a neurological basis for learning disabilities because of:
    I.   the questionable accuracy of early neurological measures.
    II.   the emphasis on behaviorism and environmentalism.
    III. the results of the use of techniques such as the MRI, PET-Scan, and fMRI.
    IV.   the validity of soft neurological signs.

    A.   I and III
    B.   I and II
    C.   II and IV
    D.   III and IV

12. Several factors have helped make professionals generally more favorably inclined toward neurological explanations of learning disabilities, including:
    I.   the decrease in the popularity of behaviorism and environmentalism.
    II.   the increase in the popularity of behaviorism and environmentalism.
    III. the increase in the utility of neurological measures.
    IV.   None of the above.

    A.   I and III
    B.   I and II
    C.   II and III
    D.   IV

13. Which of the following statements is *not* a correct description of the structure of neurons?
    A.   Dendrites are treelike projections that receive messages from the environment.
    B.   The axon is a long, tubelike extension of the neuron that carries messages to the dendrites of other neurons.
    C.   The synapse is a fatty tissue that covers and insulates axons.
    D.   Terminal buttons are structures that secrete chemicals into the synapse.

14. The occipital lobes of the cerebral cortex:
    A.   attend to attention, memory, and language production and reception.
    B.   are primarily dedicated to various aspects of visual perception.
    C.   attend to the ability to speak.
    D.   attend to the ability to comprehend language.

15. All of the following medical conditions have at times been associated with learning disabilities in young children, *except:*
    A.   premature birth.
    B.   diabetes.
    C.   cardiac arrest.
    D.   stroke.

Essay

1.   Contrast at least three historical and philosophical contributions of neurological versus behavior/environmental perspectives.

2.   Describe the major causes of learning disabilities.

3.   Discuss how different areas of the brain control different functions of a human.

4.   Explain how advances in technology have changed the way learning disabilities are being identified.

Chapter 2: Causes of Learning Disabilities

Answers To Questions

1. B (p. 44)
2. A (p. 52)
3. D (p. 56)
4. E (p. 55)
5. C (p. 43)
6. True (p. 44)
7. False (p. 50)
8. False (p. 56)
9. True (p. 57)
10. True (p. 58)
11. B (pp.44-45
12. A (p. 46)
13. C (p. 47)
14. B (p. 51)
15. D (p. 60)

Essay Grading Guidelines

1. Answers could give a historical perspective including the work of Scottish ophthalmologist James Hinshelwood, Samuel Orton, and Helmer Myklebust. The answers should explain the presumption of neurological dysfunction. Answers should then focus on the reasons why their was such a reluctance to accept neurological causes for learning disabilities such as problems of inaccurate measurement of neurological dysfunction, and the emphasis that was placed on behaviorism and environmentalism. (pp. 44)

2. Answers should fall into four different neurological dysfunction: hereditary, teratogenic, medical, and environmental factors. Heredity factors should discuss familiality, heritability, and molecular genetics. Teratogenic factors should include issues such as fetal alcohol syndrome, crack cocaine, and lead. Finally, environmental factors such as malnutrition and poor prenatal care should be explored. (pp. 56-61)

3.   Answers should give an explanation of how neurons send and receive messages. The answer should identify different parts of the brain and explain the functions of each part including the brain stem, the cerebellum, the cerebral cortex (the frontal, parietal, occipital, and temporal lobes), the left and right hemispheres, and Broca's and Wernicke's areas. (pp. 46-52)

4.   Answers should include findings from postmortem studies and neuroimaging technology (MRI, PET-Scan, and fMRI). Answers should state what the research says about dysfunction occurring most often in the left hemisphere and the growing evidence of some dysfunction in the right hemisphere as well. (pp. 54-56)

Chapter 3: Eligibility for Special Education Services

Chapter Outline

12. **What Laws Govern the Delivery of Special Education?**
    1. **IDEA - Individuals with Disabilities Education Act**
    2. **FAPE – Free and Appropriate Public Education**

13. **How is Special Education Defined?**
    1. **Definition and Practice of Special Education**
        1. **Teacher Training and Support**
        2. Class or Group Size and Composition
        3. Individualization and Teacher Direction
        4. **Assessment**
        5. **Instructional Precision**
        6. Progress Monitoring
        7. Empirical Validation
    2. Other Components of Special Education
        1. Related Services
        2. Continuum of Alternative Placements

14. How is Learning Disability Defined in IDEA?
    1. **Conceptual Definition**
        1. In General
        2. Disorders Included
        3. Disorders Not Included
    2. **Operational Definition**
    3. **Response-to-Intervention/Response-to-Treatment Approach**

15. **What is the Traditional Eligibility Process?**
    1. **Prereferral Strategies**
    2. Referral for Special Education Evaluation
    3. Evaluation
        1. Domains of Assessment
            1. Language Abilities
            2. Math Abilities
            3. Cognitive Abilities
            4. Social Skills
            5. Environmental Factors Abilities

    2. Strategies of Assessment
        1. Neuropsychological Assessment
        2. Contextual Assessment
        3. Standardized Testing
        4. Teacher-Made Tests
        5. Curriculum-Based Assessment
        6. Behavior Assessment
        7. Interactive Assessment
  4. Requirements for Evaluation Procedures
  5. Teacher's Role and Confidentiality
  6. Eligibility Decision
    1. Is This a Student with a Disability?
    2. Does This Student Need Special Education Services?

16. What is an Alternative Eligibility Process?
  1. How Does Response-to-Treatment Work?
  2. Issues Around the Response-to-Treatment Process

17. What is the Individualized Education Program?
  1. Components of the Individualized Education Program
    1. Present Level of Performance and Goals
    2. Statement of Services
    3. Participation in State- and Districtwide Assessments
    4. Transition Plan
    5. Other Components
    6. Review of the IEP
  2. Special Education Service Delivery
    1. LRE – Least Restrictive Environment
    2. Issues in Service Delivery
    3. Teaching Students in Inclusive Settings
    4. Maintaining a Continuum of Alternative Placements
    5. What Is the Effectiveness of Service Delivery Models?

Chapter 3: Eligibility for Special Education Services

Chapter Questions

Matching

_____ 1. Procedres designed to find out why a student exhibits problem behavior

_____ 2. Results in problems in speech production and/or comprehension due to a brain injury

_____ 3. Manifested in problems in math, self-regulation, and social functioning

_____ 4. The method of providing various levels of instructional intervention that become more intensive if the student does not improve in achievement level

_____ 5. A student's performance on an academic measure is significantly different than that of peers, in both level of achievement and rate of progress

A. Dual Discrepancy
B. FAPE
C. Functional Behavioral Assessment
D. Progress Monitoring
E. Response-to-Intervention

True or False

6. When special education is practiced as it should be, it is quite similar to general education along several critical dimensions of instruction, including the training and support teachers receive, class size, and precision of implementation of instructional strategies.

7. The primary law governing special education services is the Individuals with Disabilities Education Act, also known as IDEA.

8. IDEA identifies specific strategies to be used in the determination of a learning disability.

9. The IEP team includes the parents of the student, a general education teacher, a special education teacher, an LEA representative, an individual who can interpret the instruction implications of the evaluation results, others who have specific knowledge of the student, and if appropriate, the student.

10. Postsecondary goals based upon age-appropriate transition assessments must be added to

the IEP once the child reaches the age of 14.

Multiple Choice

11.   The conceptual definition of a learning disability according to IDEA includes:
    I.   a disorder in one or more of the basic psychological processes involved in understanding or in using language, spoken or written.
    II.   learning problems that are a result of visual, hearing, or motor disabilities.
    III.   emotional disturbance or mental retardation.
    IV.   conditions such as perceptual disabilities, brain injury, minimal brain dysfunction, dyslexia, and developmental aphasia.

    A.   I and IV
    B.   I and III
    C.   II and III
    D.   II and IV

12.   The traditional eligibility process to determine if a student is a student with a disability includes all of the following steps, *except*:
    A.   a referral or request for evaluation.
    B.   evaluation procedures.
    C.   eligibility determination.
    D.   a medical examination.

13.   The response-to-treatment alternative eligibility process has several potential advantages including:
    I.   identification of students using a risk rather than a deficit model.
    II.   early identification and instruction of students with learning disabilities.
    III.   reduction of identification bias.
    IV.   a strong focus on student outcomes.

    A.   I, II, and III
    B.   I, II, III and IV
    C.   I, III and IV
    D.   III and IV

14. The IEP must include a statement of:
    I.. the student's present levels of academic achievement and functional performance.
    II. measurable monthly goals.
    III. the special education and related services.
    IV. explanation about the extent to which a student will not participate with students without disabilities in the general classroom.

    A. I, II, and III
    B. I, II, III and IV
    C. I, III and IV
    D. III and IV

15. The IEP team must determine the least restrictive environment in which the student will receive special education, meaning it *must* be in:
    A. the most normal place in which appropriate education and the greatest access to the general education curriculum that is compatible with the student's needs and goals, can be offered.
    B. a general education classroom where collaborative consultation between the classroom teacher and the special education teacher occurs.
    C. a general education classroom where a general and special educator team up to teach a class together.
    D. a special education resource room where the special education teacher gives students instruction only in specific areas in which they have difficulties.

Essay

1. Explain the laws and policies that govern the delivery of special education.

2. Discuss how learning disability is defined in IDEA.

3. Describe the traditional eligibility process for determining if a student has a learning disability.

4. Assess the advantages and disadvantages of an alternative eligibility process.

5. Identify the components of an Individualized Education Program.

Chapter 3: Eligibility for Special Education Services

Answers To Questions

1.   C (p. 83)
2.   D (p. 68)
3.   B (p. 66)
4.   E (p. 71)
5.   A (p. 96)
6.   False (p. 67)
7.   True (p. 65)
8.   False (p. 85)
9.   True (p. 96)
10.   True (p. 100)
11.   A (p. 70)
12.   D (p. 73)
13.   B (p. 95)
14.   C (pp. 98-99)
15.   A (pp. 101-103)

Essay Grading Guidelines

1. Answers should describe the major points of IDEA, especially an outline of special education processes and services and the guarantee to students and their parents/guardians for a free and appropriate public education. (pp. 65-66)

2. Answer should include: specially designed instruction, no cost to the parents, meeting the unique needs of a child with a disability, special education instruction designed to address special problems in teaching and learning. It may include teacher training and support, class or group size, individualization and teacher direction, assessment, instructional precision, progress monitoring, and empirical validation. (pp. 66-68)

3. The following points should be addressed in the answers to this question: 1) teachers implement pre-referral strategies to help students before they are referred for a special education evaluation, 2) the process includes a referral, the evaluation itself (students should give the details of the evaluation), and the decision for eligibility as a student with a disability, and 3) a discussion of a variety of domains of assessment used in determining eligibility. (pp. 73-94)

4.	Answers should begin with a description of an alternative eligibility process and then move into a discussion on how response-to-treatment works as an alternative method. The student should identify and respond to issues around the response-to-treatment process. Advantages include identification of students at risk and early identification. Disadvantages include whether the model views a learning disability as "real." (pp. 94-96)

5.	Answers should define the IEP as an agreement between parents and the school about services that will be provided to a student with a disability. The IEP includes statements about the student's current performance level, annual goals for student achievement, transition plans, participation in state and district level assessments, and related services. Students should discuss the controversy surrounding the concept of full inclusion of students with disabilities, but rely on IDEA to reach a conclusion. (pp. 96-105)

Chapter 4: Parents and Family

Chapter Outline

18. **How Have Professionals' Views of Parents Changed?**
    1. **Reciprocal Effects**
    2. Passage of Federal Laws

19. **What Treatment Models Are Used with Families?**
    1. **Advocating Family-centered Models**
    2. **Family Systems Approach**
        1. **Family Characteristics**
        2. Family Interaction
        3. Family Functions
        4. Family Life Cycle
    3. Social Support Systems Approach

20. **What Are Some Current Trends in American Family Life?**
    1. **The Family Unit**
    2. **Race, Ethnicity, and Language**
    3. **Socioeconomic Status**

21. **What is the Family's Role?**
    1. **Family Adjustment**
        1. **Parental Guilt**
        2. **Parental Stress**
        3. **Sibling Reactions**
        4. **Family Reaction**
    2. **Family Values and Attitudes toward Learning**
    3. **Parents and Homework**
        1. **What Teachers Can Do**
        2. **What Parents Can Do**
        3. **What Students Can Do**

22. **How Can Communication Be Enhanced between the Family and Professionals?**
    1. Parent-Teacher Conferences
    2. School-Home Note Programs

Chapter 4: Parents and Families

Chapter Questions

Matching

_____ 1. A method used to determine the degree to which a given condition is inherited

_____ 2. The view that a person's behavior can best be understood in the context in which it occurs

_____ 3. Communication device between teacher and parent where teacher evaluates student's behavior on a form that goes home to the parent and the parent reinforces the child

_____ 4. Smaller groups from the larger group with their own unique characteristics

_____ 5. The idea that causation between child and adult behavior can go in either direction

A. Familiality Studies
B. Reciprocal Effects
C. Microcultures
D. School-Home Note Program
E. Social Systems Approach

True or False

6. The social support systems model stresses the importance of formal rather than informal sources of support for families with children with learning disabilities.

7. IDEA stipulates that parents have the right to be given opportunities to participate in meetings involving identification, evaluation, and educational placement of their child.

8. Teachers who value multi-cultural diversity respect and consider family structure and roles, values, decision-making styles, communication styles, language, and background knowledge that may differ from their own.

9. Families who have members with learning disabilities tend to adapt very well to the problems that confront them.

10. It is not critical to teach parents and students advocacy and independence skills because schools and other community agencies have procedures in place to be responsive to these students' needs. ·

Multiple Choice

11. The family systems model consists of which of the following interrelated components?
    A. family characteristics.
    B. family interaction.
    C. family functions and life cycle.
    D. All of the above.

12. How does socioeconomic status affect students with learning disabilities?
    I. Poverty places children at a greater risk of having a disability.
    II. Poverty affects how families are able to cope with a child with a disability.
    III. Families in poverty are more likely to work with school personnel.
    IV. Poverty is related to ethnic diversity in that a disproportionate number of minority families live in poverty, which in turn, stereotypes individuals with learning disabilities.

    A. I and II
    B. I, II and III
    C. I, III and IV
    D. I, II, III and IV

13. Which of the following is *least* likely to increase the chances of making homework a successful experience for students with learning disabilities?
    A. Teachers should set up a system whereby they can efficiently monitor students' homework.
    B. Teachers need to be careful that students with learning disabilities clearly understand their assignments.
    C. Teachers should give homework that reinforces previously learned material rather than the acquisition of new information.
    D. Teachers should involve parents in the homework process because of the many benefits it can yield.

14. Which of the following statements would *not* be typical of a student with a learning disability?
    A. When I do not understand an assignment or find it too hard, I seek help from my parents or siblings.
    B. After working for 30 minutes on my homework, I lose interest and quit or take a long break.
    C. I complain about homework.

D.   I need someone to do my homework with me.

15.   Teachers can use parent-teacher conferences to serve all of the following general purposes *except* to:
A.   inform parents about the student's academic and behavioral performance.
B.   gather family information in order to make an informed decision as to whether or not a student has a learning disability.
C.   plan for the student's educational program.
D.   solve problems the student may be having in school.

Essay

1.   Describe professional educators' changing views of parents.

2.   Identify the roles and responsibilities of educators and families in the assessment and educational planning process for students with learning disabilities.

3.   Describe some current trends in American family life today.

4.   Analyze the role of the family when a member has been identified with a learning disability.

5.   Create an effective model of collaboration that will foster respectful and beneficial communication between teachers and parents, given cultural perspectives and environmental characteristics.

Chapter 4: Parents and Families

Answers To Questions

1. A (p. 119)
2. E (p. 112)
3. D (p. 135)
4. C (p. 116)
5. B (p. 110)
6. False (p. 115)
7. True (p. 111)
8. True (p. 117)
9. True (p. 121)
10. False (p. 126)
11. D (pp. 113-115)
12. C (p. 117)
13. C (pp. 123-124)
14. A (p. 125)
15. B (p. 130)

Essay Grading Guidelines

1. Answers should show how professionals' views of parents have changed from negative perspectives to more positive perspectives. Professionals once placed blame on parents for their children's problems. Now they view them more positively due to two factors: 1) research findings demonstrate the principle of reciprocal effects and Congressional mandates that parents have more opportunities to be involved. (pp. 109-111)

2. Answers should show how current trends are characterized by family-centered approaches and stressing social systems. Two of these approaches are: 1) the Turnbulls' family system model (family characteristics, family interaction, family function, family life cycle) and 2) Dunst's social support systems model (informal sources of support). (pp. 111-116)

3. Answers should show how microcultures are becoming more diverse in the areas of the family unit, race, ethnicity, language, and socioeconomic status. Answers should also talk about the implications these changes have on the field of learning disabilities. (pp. 116-117)

4.   Answers should give this historical perspective on family reaction in which a stage theory (such as that of the stages of death) was used to explain family reactions to having a child with a disability. From there the answers should identify the two reaction that parents typically have: guilt and stress. Siblings all might express stress. Answers should point out that most families adjust well with only minor difficulties. Family values and attitudes toward learning affect students. Homework is a major area of concern so answers should point out how homework should be handled by the teacher, the parents, and the student. (pp. 117-121)

5.   Answers to this question will vary, nonetheless, they should include a clear indication on how to prepare for the two most common methods of parent-teacher communication (parent-teacher conferences and school-home note programs). (pp. 130-136)

Chapter 5: Prevention and Intervention in Early Childhood

Chapter Outline

23. How Can Learning Disabilities Be Prevented?
1. Primary Prevention
2. Secondary Prevention
3. Tertiary Prevention
4. **Addressing Risk Factors in Infancy and Early Childhood**
5. Distinguishing Disabilities from Cultural Differences and Normal Variations

24. How Are Learning Disabilities Identified in Infancy and Early Childhood?
1. Two Approaches to Early Identification
    1. Generic Approach
    2. Specific Approach
2. Promises and Pitfalls of Early Identification

25. How is Early Childhood Intervention Provided?
1. **Popular Early Intervention Programs**
    1. **Project Head Start**
    2. **Reading Recovery**
    3. **Success for All**
2. **Legal Requirements of Early Intervention**
3. **Evaluating Early Childhood Program Quality**

26. What Are Some Trends in Early Childhood Special Education?
1. **Inclusive Education**
2. DAP - Developmentally Appropriate Practices
3. Education for Transition
4. Family-Based Education
5. Assessment
6. Self-Determination
7. Technology

Chapter 5: Prevention and Intervention in Early Childhood

Chapter Questions

Matching

_____ 1.   A behavioral style of responding to people and situations

_____ 2.   An educational program that is appropriate for the student's age and needs

_____ 3.   A term used to describe a variety of disabilities of young children

_____ 4.   People from other cultures or having a native language other than the dominant group

_____ 5.   Keeping the effects of the problem or disability from spreading to other areas of functioning

A.   CLD
B.   DAP
C.   Developmentally Delayed
D.   Temperament
E.   Tertiary Prevention

True or False

6.   It is too late to use primary prevention once problems have emerged.

7.   Learning disabilities are usually detected before the child enters school.

8.   Project Head Start, Reading Recovery, and Success for All are three nationally known early intervention programs.

9.   Self-determination, the making of one's own decisions about important aspects of life, is a trend in thinking about all people with disabilities.

10.   Computer-assisted instruction (CID) is not an effective teaching tool for students with learning disabilities because these children need more of a personal interaction with an individual such as a teacher or mentor.

11. Adverse conditions that may put children at high risk for learning disabilities include all of the following, *except:*
    A. poverty, poor nutrition , and exposure to environmental conditions.
    B. teenage mother, particularly mothers in their middle and late teens.
    C. abuse, neglect, and an environment in which violence and substance abuse are pervasive.
    D. cuts in social programs that widen the gap between the needs of children and families and the availability of social services.

12. Promises of early identification of learning disabilities includes:
    A. helping students cope with any potential stigma and anxiety created by the identification of a learning disability.
    B. putting effort into the prevention of learning disabilities.
    C. providing children with programs in the preschool years so they can experience academic achievement once they enter school.
    D. the common wisdom that it will be followed by early intervention.

13. The IFSL is similar to the IEP in that it must include:
    I.   present levels of the child's cognitive, physical, language and speech, psycho-social, and self-help development.
    II.   major expected outcomes for the child and family.
    III. projected dates for initiating and ending the services.
    IV.   name of the case manager.

    A. I and IV
    B. II, III, and IV
    C. I, II, III, and IV
    D. III and IV

14. Trends in the early twenty-first century in early childhood special education include:
    I.   exclusion of young children with disabilities in preschools serving normally developing youngsters.
    II.   practices described as developmentally appropriate.
    III. traditional approaches to the assessment of young children.
    IV.   self-determination of young children with disabilities.

    A. II and IV
    B. I and III
    C. II and III
    D. I and IV

15. Family-based education is highly desirable because:
    A. much of early education is grounded in the home.
    B. the variety found in families' language and literacy traditions, views of disability, assumptions about learning, and ways of relating to school personnel help teachers accept and understand the reality of cultural differences.
    C. families differ tremendously in what they need and what they can do.
    D. All of the above.

Essay

1. Describe how learning disabilities can be prevented.

2. Discuss how learning disabilities are identified in infancy and early childhood.

3. Identify how early childhood intervention is provided.

4. Assess the effectiveness of several trends in early childhood education.

5. Describe how special educators can demonstrate a commitment to understanding diverse cultures and language, and be sensitive to the many aspects of diversity.

Chapter 5: Prevention and Intervention in Early Childhood

Answers To Questions

1. D (p. 148)
2. B (p. 158)
3. C (p. 150)
4. A (p. 147)
5. E (p. 144)
6. True (p. 144)
7. False (p. 149)
8. True (p. 153)
9. True (p. 161)
10. False (p. 162)
11. B (p. 146)
12. D (p. 151)
13. C (p. 155)
14. A (p. 156)
15. A (p. 159)

Essay Grading Guidelines

1. Answers should show how prevention may be primary (keeping disabilities from occurring at all), secondary (correcting a problem or keeping it from growing worse), and tertiary (keeping the problem from spreading to other areas). Answers may address risk factors for learning disabilities in infancy and early childhood. Answers should also distinguish learning disabilities and cultural differences. (pp. 144-148)

2. Answers should discuss both a generic approach and a specific approach to identify learning disabilities. A generic approach give a general designation while a specific approach giving specific labels. Students should discuss the advantages and disadvantages of early identification including the promise of prevention vs. the pitfall of misidentification. (pp. 149-152)

3. Answers should describe popular early intervention programs like Project Head Start, Reading Recovery, and Success for All. Project Head Start: a preschool program for disadvantaged youngsters. Reading Recovery: a reading tutorial program. Success for All: a program designed for disadvantaged primary-grade children. Answers should also identify the legal requirements of early intervention (IDEA and other federal laws). Answers should discuss the guidelines for evaluating early childhood program quality

including questions relevant to general and special education, the way a child feels about the program, and family and community involvement. (pp. 152-156)

4. Answers should discuss the following trends: 1) greater inclusion of young children with disabilities, 2) the acceptance of practices described as developmentally appropriate, 3) new approaches to the assessment of young children, 4) emphasis on transition of children from home to preschool to kindergarten, and 5) emphasis on family involvement. Other trends that may be discussed include self-determination and the use of technology. (pp. 156-163)

5. Answers will vary. Answers should address the relationship among culture, language and reading. (p. 160)

Chapter 6: Transition Programming in Adolescence and Adulthood

Chapter Outline

27.   What are Learning Disability Outcomes Across the Life Span?
1. Higher Dropout Rates
   1. Encouraging trends, still more likely to drop out
2. Higher Underemployment
   1. Hold jobs that are below their level
   2. Less likely to attend post secondary school, less earning potential
3. Greater Dependency on Others
   1. After high school, living with relatives

28.   What Transition Programs and Services Are Available?
1. Federal Initiatives
   1. IDEA (passes in 1990, amended in 1997)
2. Interagency Collaboration and Service Delivery
   1. Vocational Rehabilitation Personnel
   2. College Learning Disabilities Specialist
3. Social Skills and Self-Advocacy Training
   1. Necessary skills difficult to define
   2. Skills not easily trained
   3. Important in order for success
   4. Advocacy as part of training in order to articulate needs
4. Parent Involvement
   1. Precareer activities
   2. Honor choices to increase independence
   3. Develop sources of support
   4. Foster independency by providing support and guidance
5. Vocational Training and College Preparation
   1. Orientation of transition program is biggest challenge
   2. Advantage in determining direction early

29.   How are Students with Learning Disabilities Prepared for College?
1. Programming Goals for College Preparation
   1. Content general education courses
   2. Special education consultation to general education
   3. Special education for survival skills
   4. Interaction with counselor
   5. Evenly spaced graduation courses

30.   How Can Students with Learning Disabilities Succeed in College?
1. Guidelines for Choosing a College
   1. Entrance requirements

        2.   Curricula requirements
        3.   Learning disabilities services
  2.   Predictors of Success in College
        1.   No established research base
        2.   Admissions look at high school performance
        3.   Other factors, motivation and independence
  3.   Instructional Accommodations
        1.   Adjustments to course requirements
        2.   Modifications in program requirements
        3.   Auxiliary aids
        4.   Departments define essential requirements

31.   How Can Students with Learning Disabilities Prepare for the Work World?
  1.   Programming Goals for Vocational Training
        1.   Career awareness
        2.   Career exploration
        3.   Career experiences
  2.   School-Business Partnerships
        1.   Help businesses prepare personnel
        2.   Issue of tracking too early
        3.   Advantage of students having access to job training

32.   How Can Employers Encourage Success for Adults with Learning Disabilities?
  1.   Workplace Accommodations
        1.   Functional limitations
        2.   Understanding job requirements

VII.   How Can Employees with Learning Disabilities Succeed in the Workplace?
  A.   Choose a job that is a good match
        1.   Understanding of one's disability
  2.   Use Personal Contacts to Find a Job
        1.   Getting one's foot in the door
  3.   Become a Self-Advocate
        1.   How one's disability affects performance
  4.   Develop Compensatory Strategies
        1.   Extra time, rechecking, extra efforts
  5.   Take Advantage of Technology
        1.   Tied to functions that need to be performed
        2.   Intuitive to learn
        3.   Supported by hot lines
        4.   High benefit/cost ratio
  6.   Gain Control over One's Life
        1.   Reframe

Chapter 6: Transition Programming in Adolescence and Adulthood

Chapter Questions

True or False

1.   Both vocational rehabilitation personnel and college representatives might be involved in the IEP transition process.

2.   Since the federal law initiating transition for students in special education was passed, educational services have been quick to respond with the teaching of self-advocacy and interagency collaboration involvement.

3.   Professionals should especially strive for positive relationships with culturally and linguistically diverse parents because research tells us there is a discrepancy of views toward transition involvement between parents and educators.

4.   College bound students in special education should take courses in survival skills and should receive their "content" area courses from special education teachers.

5.   Part of reframing includes understanding the limitations of ones' disability; a necessary component to successful employment.

Multiple Choice

6.   Which item is *not* accurate when examining outcomes for children with learning disabilities across their lifespan:
    A.   higher rates of dropping out in secondary school.
    B.   greater dependency on others, independent living.
    C.   intensive programming at the elementary and secondary levels can "cure" the disability.
    D.   underemployment, long-run earning potential is likely to be significantly less.

7.   The first federal legislation Congress passed mandating schools to provide transition services for all students with disabilities was:
    A.   P.L. 94-142 in 1975, Education for All Handicapped Children Act.
    B.   P.L. 101-476 in 1990, IDEA.
    C.   P.L. 100-20, in 1999, amendment to IDEA.
    D.   1999, Americans with Disabilities Act.

8. Federal law requires that a transition plan:
   A. replace the Individualized Educational Program with an Individualized Transition Plan.
   B. begin at age 12 with statements of transition service needs to be annually included in a child's Individualized Program focusing on courses of study such as advanced placement or vocational education.
   C. begin at age 16 with statements of transition services as determined by the Individualized Program team including interagency responsibilities.
   D. is concluded by the age of 18.

9. One of the biggest challenges facing students with learning disabilities, their parents, and their teachers is to:
   A. involve interagency collaboration and service delivery in order to ensure transition outcomes and guard against service duplication.
   B. teach social skills as part of academic curriculum.
   C. foster student independence through self-advocacy training.
   D. decide if the student's transition program should be oriented towards vocational training or college preparation.

10. Today, it is possible for individuals with learning disabilities to attend college and be successful because:
   A. of the passage of Section 504 of the Rehabilitation Act of 1973, which has helped define the parameters of the law in accommodating students.
   B. institutions of higher education are required to provide centers devoted to services for students with learning disabilities.
   C. admissions officers can predict student success based upon GPAs and SATs or ACTs for students with learning disabilities.
   D. program faculty have clearly identified essential components and appropriate accommodations.

11. One reason school-work training programs for students with learning disabilities have *not* been widely adopted in the United States is because:
   A. most vocational specialists do not promote the idea as beneficial for non-college bound students.
   B. area businesses usually do not view the partnership as beneficial to their "bottom line".
   C. a reticence to identify individuals in schools for a non-college-bound-track too early in their educational career.
   D. educational structures unwillingness to provide academic credit for work experience.

12.   There are specific workplace trends that have created less than optimistic employment concerns for individuals with learning disabilities. Which of the following is *not* one of these trends?
    A.   Bureaucratic, hierarchical structures are being replaced by teamwork environments.
    B.   Technology innovations are being introduced into the workplace at a rapid pace.
    C.   Travel requires increased independence, self-assurance, and mobility across cultures.
    D.   Standardized credentialing and licensing examinations are increasing.

13.   Self-advocacy as it relates to employment is:
    A.   often linked to effective social skills when approaching the matter of disability self-revelation.
    B.   unnecessary at the high school level because teachers and counselors can work together to identify a career path for an individual student.
    C.   best fulfilled by someone other than the individual with the learning disability once employment begins.
    D.   a cooperative responsibility, as protected by law, between the individual and the employer.

14.   If you were a special education teacher, you could use what computer-based assistive technology to help students with learning disabilities to compensate for spelling deficits?
    A.   outlining and brainstorming programs.
    B.   word prediction software.
    C.   personal data managers.
    D.   electronic reference materials.

15.   What is the single most important thing an individual with a learning disability can do to ensure employment success?
    A.   desire success.
    B.   be motivated to achieve success.
    C.   have strong personal and professional networks.
    D.   reframe the disability through psychological and emotional control.

Essay

1.   Define what transition means in terms of "quality of life perspective".

2.   When developing individualized transition plans for students, who should be involved, and what are the critical components? Explain rationales for the answers you give.

3.   What are the pros and cons of placing (including potential outcomes) a student with a learning disability in a college preparation program versus a vocational training program?

Examine this issue from 3 perspectives, that of the student, the special education teacher, and the parent(s).

4. Given the recent workplace trends and current federal law, describe how individuals with learning disabilities can obtain quality jobs, self-advocate for what needed accommodations, and remain viable in their employment.

5. If you were the special education teacher in a high school, responsible for teaching English, what computer-based assistive technology would you seek to use in your classroom to prepare your students for success in post-secondary settings? Give rationales for your choices.

Chapter 6: Transition Programming in Adolescence and Adulthood

Answers To Questions

1. True (p. 172)
2. False (p. 173) answer is "slow"
3. True (p. 174)
4. False (p. 176)
5. True (p. 190)
6. C (pp. 168-169)
7. B (p. 169)
8. C (p. 170)
9. D (p. 175)
10. A (pp. 176-177)
11. C (p. 183)
12. C (p. 183)
13. A (p. 187)
14. B (p. 189)
15. D (p. 190)

Essay Grading Guidelines

1. Answers must stress that transition is not just about employment. It includes post-secondary education, becoming involved in a community, and experiencing satisfactory personal and social relationships. It must involve coordination of interagency services including the student and focus on independence, happiness, and fulfillment. (pp. 167-168)

2. Answers should include special education teacher, general education teacher (if the student is receiving any of their education in general education classes), vocational rehabilitation counselor, college representative, student case manager, the student, and possibly the parent(s). Rationales for including these individuals is to inform the student and the family of all services and expectations from various educational settings. Critical components will include personal needs, interests, and preferences with interagency linkages. (pp. 170-172)

3. Answers should address the issue of tracking students too early into a vocational orientation or a college prep set of course work. Some students may be pressured by parents to go to college and in doing so, be unsuccessful. On the other hand, some students may be placed in vocational course work when they have the potential to obtain a college degree. If students are allowed to participate in vocational training programs in high school, it allows them opportunities to obtain employment in high school and during the summer months. (pp. 183-185)

4.   Answers should include information about choosing a job that utilizes a person's strengths, cultivating and using personal networks to "get one's foot in the door", using extreme caution when self-advocating for "reasonable accommodations" (such as see p. 185 for listing), gaining control over one's life by reframing, and engaging in continual learning to meet the demands of greater productivity. (pp. 183-191)

5.   Answers to this question will vary, nonetheless, they should include a clear indication on which assistive technology they would use and it should be appropriate for an English classroom. They should also provide clear rationales for why they would be using the technology in this setting as it relates to preparing students to be successful in post-secondary settings. For example the use of a personal data manager would clearly be appropriate as many assignments will be given with different deadlines, and students will need to learn how to manage deadlines independently in post-secondary settings. (pp. 188-189)

Chapter 7: Social, Emotional, and Behavioral Problems

Chapter Outline

33. What is the Link Between Learning Disabilities and Social, Emotional, and Behavioral Problems?
    1. Social Competence
        1. Effective use of social skills
        2. Absence of maladaptive behavior
        3. Positive relations with others
        4. Accurate, age-appropriate social cognition
    2. Conduct Problems
        1. Overt antisocial behavior (aggression, tantrums, disruption)
        2. Covert antisocial behavior (lying, stealing)
    3. Other Social, Emotional, and Behavioral Problems
        1. Anxiety, depression, hopeless

34. What Are the Major Causes of Social, Emotional, and Behavioral Problems?
    1. Schooling as a Possible Cause
        1. Instruction: first defense
        2. Expectations: fits level of ability
        3. Tolerance: balance between conformity and acceptable difference
        4. Reinforcement: positive, frequent, immediate
        5. Consistency: structure, firm expectations, consequences
        6. Models: call attention to and reward imitation

35. How Should We Access the Characteristics of Social, Emotional, and Behavioral Problems? (internalizing and externalizing behaviors)
    1. Screening
        1. Process of eliminating or confirming a problem
        2. Series of steps successively narrowed
        3. Systematic Screening for Behavior Disorders
        4. Take into account cultural differences
    2. Prereferral Interventions
        1. Document management strategies used
    3. Social, Emotional, and Behavioral Problems in IEP Development
        1. Information from multiple sources
        2. Plan a program to change behavior
    4. Functional Behavioral Assessment and Behavior Intervention Plans
        1. Function of the behavior
        2. Precorrection-find ways of altering circumstances to teach behavior
        3. Proactive Behavior Intervention Plan
    5. Other Possible Legal Aspects of Dealing with Behavior
        1. Manifestation determination

36. What Are the Main Educational Methods Used for Social, Emotional, and Behavioral Problems?
1. Modifying the Learning Environment for Proactive Management
    1. Best proactive strategy is effective academic instruction with frequent student correct responses and low error rates
    2. Evaluate the context: precorrect by examination of problem situations
    3. Share expected behavior: precorrect by teaching the behaviors desired
    4. Modify the context: precorrect by changing the context to avert misbehavior
    5. Involve student in rehearsal: precorrect by practicing the expected behavior
    6. Reinforce performance: providing a satisfying consequence
    7. Prompts or signals: help a student to remember "do it now"
    8. Monitoring plan: systematic, direct, recording of progress
2. Teaching Desired Behavior
    1. Early intervention (before misconduct becomes serious)
    2. Instructions (simple, clear, firm, polite)
    3. Models (reinforcement for imitating)
    4. Choices (meaningful, structured)
    5. Positive reinforcement (choice, immediacy, frequency)
    6. Social skills (extensive modeling and practice)
3. Discouraging Undesired Behavior
    1. Correcting requires Teaching
    2. Punishing consequences are often highly rewarding
    3. Response cost (withdrawing a privilege)
    4. Positive reinforcement of alternative behavior (replacing with expected)

Chapter 7: Social, Emotional, and Behavioral Problems

Chapter Questions

Matching

_____ 1. A classroom environment that is balanced
             between compliance to necessary rules
             and acceptance of differences

_____ 2. Instructions are clearly provided to
             students with firm expectations and
             dependable consequences for behavior

_____ 3. Clarity of the task, opportunities to respond
             frequently, sequential presentation of tasks,
             relevance to everyday life, and frequent
             measurement of performance

_____ 4. Adjusting performance prospects to fit
             a student's ability in order to promote
             challenge and success

_____ 5. Call attention to the behavior which should
             be imitated and reward imitation of these
             representations of desired behaviors

_____ 6. Rewards provided frequently, immediately,
             interestingly, and contingent upon desired
             behaviors combined with knowing when
             and how to ignore negative behavior

A. Models
B. Reinforcement
C. Consistency
D. Instruction
E. Tolerance
F. Expectations

True or False

7. Students with learning disabilities are able to "read" social situation and understand how other are trying to influence them.

8. Research suggests that receiving education in a separate education in a separate setting has a positive effect, if any, on self-esteem.

9. Teachers should consider how their own behavior might be contributing to a student's misbehavior.

10. Screening for social, emotional, and behavioral problems should depend on one person's opinions and interpretations to control for errors in identification which could be caused by cultural differences.

11. Manifestation determination, a controversial issue, decides if a behavior is the result of a disability or not and then influences disciplinary action.

Multiple Choice

12. Which of the following statements is true concerning students with learning disabilities?
    A. As many as 50% of individuals labeled learning disabled could be formally diagnosed with another label.
    B. Students with learning disabilities present behavior management problems that are similar to typical students.
    C. All individuals with learning disabilities will exhibit social and behavioral problems.
    D. For some students with learning disabilities, the social domain is an area of strength.

13. Causes of problem behaviors for individuals with learning disabilities:
    A. are often identified early by educators in an effort to prevent further risks.
    B. are nearly always due to a single identifiable factor.
    C. may be partly biological, partly familial, partly due to educational mismanagement, and partly cultural.
    D. is not an obligation or responsibility of schools and educators.

14. Assessment of emotional and behavioral problems should:
    A. be solution centered.
    B. rely on one person's judgement.
    C. be based on speculation about functionality.
    D. focus entirely on the student's behaviors.

15. Punishment is:
    A. a replacement for teaching expected behaviors.
    B. a fine levied for inappropriate behaviors.
    C. providing reinforcement for and acceptable incompatible behavior.
    D. often highly rewarding for some students.

Essay

1. Explain how social competence, conduct, and other emotional/behavioral problems can contribute to a cycle of academic failure for individuals with learning disabilities.

2. What is an FBA and how can it help students? What tool(s) are needed to change behavior?

3.   Describe the seven step proactive approach for behavior management devised by Colvin, Sugai, and Patching, which addresses precorrection. Explain how this compares with technology of instruction.

4.   Why are choices important to positive reinforcement? And how can both be used in discouraging undesired behavior?

5.   Why has research on social skills training proven so ineffective? What are the necessary elements of social skills training if it is going to make a difference in the lives of individuals with learning disabilities?

Chapter 7: Social, Emotional, and Behavioral Problems

Answers to Questions

20.   E (pp. 200-201)
21.   C (pp. 200-201)
22.   D(pp. 200-201)
23.   F (pp. 200-201)
24.   A (pp. 200-201)
25.   B (pp. 200-201)
26.   False (p. 197)
27.   True (p. 198)
28.   True (p. 200)
29.   False (pp. 203-204)
30.   True (p. 206)
31.   D (p. 196)
32.   C (pp. 199-200)
33.   A (pp. 202-203)
34.   D (p. 217)

Essay Grading Guidelines

1.   Answers should present information about the 4 components of social competence and how these interact with self-concept and attributions for academic failure. Additionally, information should indicate the reciprocal nature between academic failure and social behavioral problems. (pp. 196-199)

2.   Answers should detail how a Functional Behavioral Assessment can be used to determine the purpose or function of a behavior. The student can then be taught how to achieve the same goal using a different behavior. This activity can be achieved using a Proactive Behavior Management Plan with precorrection rather than punishment. (pp. 204-206)

3.   Answers should include 7 items: Evaluate the context, State expected behavior, Modify the context, Involve the student in rehearsal, Reinforce correct performance, Use prompts or signals, and Establish a monitoring plan. Additional information regarding technology should state that techniques are like computer software, anticipating (precorrection) and responding to behavior with consistency and precision. (pp. 280-286)

4.   Answers should include information about choices needing to be meaningful and structured and that choices for students can be part of a positive reinforcement determination. Information about positive reinforcement should include that it must be immediate and frequent. It also can be used for reinforcing a desirable behavior over an undesirable behavior. (pp. 214 & 219)

5.   Information presented must indicate that research on training has been brief, may have been given to students who are already socially skilled, may not have followed well-designed or field-tested curriculum, and may have only focused on social skills deficits rather than on low achievement which is a variable in poor self-esteem and thus peer rejection and social skills. Elements of training need to include use of systemic, prolonged, field-tested curriculum combined with instruction to address academic failure. Children should be provided modeling, prompting of appropriate skills, and extensive opportunities to practice. (p. 216)

Chapter 8: Cognition, Metacognition, and Memory in Students with Learning Disabilities

Chapter Outline

37. How Can We Explain Learning and Memory?
1. **Information Processing Theory**
   1. **Short-Term Memory**
   2. Working Memory
   3. Long-Term Memory
   4. **Executive Control or Metacognitive Processes**
   5. **Motivation**

38. What do We Know about the Learning and Memory of Students with Learning Disabilities?
1. **Learning Styles**
   1. **Review of research yields student gains are "very little" when taught to their learning style**
   2. Little evidence that learning styles can be assessed adequately or used effectively for instruction
2. Cognitive Styles
   1. **Field dependence-heavily influenced by their environment; Field independence-focus on the most essential data (children with LD are often more field dependent)**
   2. Reflectivity versus Impulsivity (children with LD tend to be more impulsive)
3. Memory Styles
   1. **Short-Term Memory (children with LD demonstrate significant auditory short-term memory problems when compared to nondisabled peers)**
   2. Working Memory (children with LD have problems with working memory and executive function that integrates the long-term and working memory)
4. Metacognitive or Executive Control Abilities
   1. **Metamemory-ability to think about memory strategies**
   2. Metalistening-**ability to conceptualize the listening process**
   3. Metacomprehension-**ability to think about how one understands**
5. Motivation
   1. **External Locus of Control (children with LD tend to have an external locus of control)**
   2. Negative Attributions (**self-efficacy beliefs**)
   3. Learned Helplessness (**inactive learners-cycle of failure**)

39. How Can Learning, Memory, and Motivation Needs be Addressed?
    1. **Self- Instruction**
        1. Verbalizing the steps in a task
        2. Proven effective but not a "cure all"
        3. Specific guidelines provided **(consistency, continued practice, and generalization needed)**
    2. **Self-Monitoring of Academic Performance**
        1. **Academic gains in productivity and accuracy**
        2. Limited to skills the student may already posses (in their repertoire)
    3. **Self-Determination**
    4. Mnemonic Strategies
        1. **Keyword**
        2. Pegword
        3. Reconstructive elaborations
    5. Attribution Training
        1. **Mixed results-best way to turn student motivation around is to make sure they experience success**
    6. Cognitive Strategies (when to use, how to use, how to determine success)
        1. **Test-Taking (PIRATES, Hughes, 1996)**
        2. Content Textbook **(Rooney, 1998)**
        3. Sometimes difficult to get students to learn and use
        4. Students must have prerequisite skills necessary
    7. General Teaching Practices to Activate Learning and Memory
        1. **Advance organizers**
        2. Activate background knowledge
        3. Organization explicit to aid storage and retrieval
        4. Continuous feedback and distributed practice
        5. Dialogue in how you learn
        6. Communicate appropriate expectations
        7. Engage students in learning to use working memory and executive function
        8. Assistive Technology (ABCs)

Chapter 8: Cognition, Metacognition, and Memory in Students with Learning Disabilities

---

Chapter Questions

Matching

_____ 1.   Ability to think.

_____ 2.   Ability to think about thinking

_____ 3.   Learning initiative and independence

_____ 4.   Ability to think about how one
                  understands

A.   Metacomprehension
B.   Cognition
C.   Metacognition
D.   Self-regulation

True or False

5.   Schemata is an organized interconnected series of memories in long-term memory that is used to link onto new knowledge.

6.   Learning Styles can be adequately assessed and used effectively for instruction.

7.   Self-instruction, as a cognitive training technique, can be considered as a "cure all" for many learning problems.

8.   Self-monitoring improves academic productivity and accuracy.

9.   An appropriate assistive technology tool for an individual with needs in the area of math would be to provide an electronic organizer.

Short Answer

10.   How is information moved from a "teacher's verbal directions" to short term memory?

          _____.

11.   What is the function of short term memory?

          _____

_____.

12.   _____ _____ oversees the information processing system. Its main

functions are _____ _____, _____ _____, and

_____ _____.

13.   When students with learning disabilities wait for others to motivate and organize their lives,

it is called _____ _____ ____ _____.

14.   Cognitive training involves: (1) _____ _____ _____,

(2) _____ _____ ____ _____, and (3) _____

_____-_____.

15.   Two out of the list of seven techniques that teachers can use to help students with learning

disabilities better develop their learning capabilities are _____ and

_____.

Essay

1.   Describe the process of "working memory".

2.   How is information stored and associated in "long-term memory"?

3.   What is more important, short-term memory problems or working memory and executive
functioning problems and why?

4.   For a student with a learning disability, how does the "cycle of failure" impact the ability to
achieve academic success?

5.   1) What is a mnemonic strategy? 2) Why is it effective? 3) Pick one example and explain
how it is used.

Chapter 8: Cognition, Metacognition, and Memory in Students with Learning Disabilities

Answers To Questions

1.   B (pp. 223-224)
2.   C (pp. 223-224)
3.   D (pp. 223-224)
4.   A (pp. 223-224)
5.   True (p. 225)
6.   False (p. 230)
7.   False (p. 241)
8.   True (p. 242)
9.   False (p. 253)
10.   By student attention to the information (p. 224)
11.   Holds information or passes it to working memory (p. 224)
12.   Executive control; task analysis, strategy control, and strategy monitoring (p. 225)
13.   external locus of control (p. 236)
14.   1) changing thought processes, 2) providing strategies for learning, and 3) teaching self-initiative (p. 238)
15.   Two out of the following: provide advance organizers, activate prior knowledge, organize material explicitly, provide continuous feedback and distributed practice, dialogue on how you learn, communicate appropriate expectations, engage in active learning (p. 251)

Essay Grading Guidelines

1.   Connect incoming information to long-term storage (p. 224)
     · Chunking
     · Clustering
     · Rehearsing
Information can be lost
     · Interference
     · Displacement
     · Decay
Information held for short periods of time

2.   Episodic memory (p. 225)
             Images organized by space and time
       Semantic memory
             Facts and skills and how to use them
       Procedural memory

Automatic information

3.   Working memory ability predict reading comprehension task performance. (pp. 233-234) Students with LD have problems integrating long-term working memory, thus it takes longer to complete tasks leading to less success.

4.   Answers should include most of the following: external locus of control; negative attributions; learned helplessness; inactive learners; cognitive, metacognitive, or motivational problems combine to make them passive in the face of needed involved learning. (pp. 236-237)

5.   1) A visual or acoustic representations to enhance memory and retrieval.
2) Remember better if they can use concrete cues and draw on prior knowledge.
3) Keyword, pegword, reconstructive elaboration. Examples found on (pp. 245-246)

Chapter 9: Attention Deficit Hyperactive Disorder

Chapter Outline

40. What Are the Links between Learning Disabilities and Attention Problems?

41. What Are the Historical Origins of ADHD?
    1. Early Observations of ADHD symptoms
    2. The Strauss Syndrome
    3. The Bridge from Mental Retardation to Normal Intelligence
    4. Minimal Brain Injury and the Hyperactive Child Syndrome

42. What is Today's Definition of ADHD?

43. What is the Prevalence of ADHD?

44. How is ADHD Assessed?
    1. Medical Exam
    2. Clinical Interview
    3. Rating Scales
    4. Using Technology to Assess ADHD
    5. Issues Related to Identification for Special Education Services

45. What Are the Causes of ADHD?
    1. Neurological Factors
    2. Hereditary Factors
    3. Factors that Don't Cause ADHD

46. What Are the Behavioral Characteristics of Persons with ADHD?
    1. Barkley's Model of ADHD: Behavioral Inhibition and Time Awareness and Management

47. What Educational Methods Are Used with Students with ADHD?
    1. Stimulus Reduction
    2. Structure
    3. Functional Behavior Assessment
    4. Contingency-Based Self-Management
    5. Self-Monitoring of Attention

48. What is the Role of Medication for Persons with ADHD?
    1. Side Effects
    2. Negative Publicity Regarding Ritalin
    3. Research on the Effectiveness of Medication
    4. Cautions Regarding Ritalin

Chapter 9: Attention Deficit Hyperactivity Disorder

Chapter Questions

Matching

_____ 1. An executive function; internal language   A. Rating Scales
used to regulate one's behavior; delayed   B. Working Memory
or impaired in those with ADHD   C. Educational Methods used
                with ADHD students

_____ 2. The most commonly prescribed   D. 3% to 5%
psychostimulant for ADHD   E. Inner Speech
         F. Ritalin

_____ 3. Used as a method of evaluation to obtain
more objective, behavioral data

_____ 4. Stimulus Reduction, Structure, Functional
Behavior Assessment, Contingency-Based
Self-Management and Self-Monitoring of
Attention are all part of

_____ 5. Percentage of school-age children are
Diagnosed with ADHD in the United States

_____ 6. The ability to remember information while also
performing other cognitive operations

True or False

7. If a student has ADHD, then the student should be labeled learning disabled.

8. Children exhibit their worst behavior at the doctor's office known as Doctor's Office
Effect.

9. In the 1970's Benjamin Feingold introduced the theory that certain food additives caused
hyperactivity in children.

10. It is a known fact that too early of use of psychostimulants in children can cause them to
turn to drugs in their teen years.

11. There is strong evidence that hereditary factors are the cause of many cases of ADHD.

Multiple Choice

12. Which one of the following is not seen as links between learning disabilities and attention problems?
    A. 20% of students with learning disabilities are also diagnosed as ADHD.
    B. Outbreak of encephalitis in 1917 left many children with symptoms of inattention.
    C. Some students with learning disabilities who are not formally identified as ADHD also have attention problems that affect their learning.
    D. Learning disability may precede the attention problems, the attention problems may precede learning disability, or the attention problems and learning disabilities may be conditions that co-occur.

13. Researchers have pointed which of the following as being structurally smaller and reducing blood flow in individuals with ADHD:
    A. their feet.
    B. prefrontal and frontal lobes in front of the brain.
    C. cerebellum.
    D. neurotransmitters.

14. Today's definition of ADHD:
    A. ability to focus on relevant features of a task without being distracted by irrelevant aspects.
    B. boys and girls who cannot sit down and like to run around the room.
    C. points to symptoms that include failing to attend to details, disorganized, does not follow through with tasks, acts as though not listening when spoken to, forgets things, talks non-stop.
    D. child who displays overt antisocial behavior, such as aggression, tantrums, and disruption, covert antisocial behavior, such as lying and stealing.

15. Authorities recommend that a diagnosis of ADHD should include which three elements?
    A. Shot record, clinical interview or history, behavior notes.
    B. Medical examination, clinical interview or history, administration of teacher and parent rating scales.
    C. Medical examination, behavior notes, parent observation.
    D. Ritalin, shot record, clinical interview, parent and teacher rating scales.

16. Causes of ADHD are:
    A. poor home life and parenting skills.
    B. heredity, neurological factors.
    C. small pox and encephalitis outbreaks.
    D. food additives and too much sugar.

Essay

1. Do you think there is gender bias in identifying students with ADHD?

2. What are the three elements of behavioral inhibition? What is the educator's goal in regard to these elements?

3. What educational methods are used with students with ADHD?

4. Why is it important for you to pay attention to the possible side effects of students taking psychostimulants?

Chapter 9: Attention Deficit Hyperactivity Disorder

Answers to Questions

35.   E (p. 279)
36.   F (p. 286)
37.   A(p. 268)
38.   C (pp. 280-286)
39.   D (pp. 265-267)
40.   B (pp. 278-279)
41.   False (pp. 259-260)
42.   False (pp. 267)
43.   True (pp. 275-276)
44.   False (pp. 286-287)
45.   True (p. 275)
46.   B (p. 261)
47.   B (pp. 270-274)
48.   C (pp. 263-264)
49.   B (pp. 267-269)
50.   B (pp. 270-274)

Essay Grading Guidelines

1.   Answers should include information from the National Institutes of Health. Answers should include information relevant to why boys are labeled ADHD more than girls according to Barkley. Also mention of discrepancy of underidentification of girls. (pp. 265-266)

2.   Answers should include Barkley's Model fo ADHD, also include executive functions, working memory, and inner speech. (pp. 277-280)

3.   Answers should include Stimulus Reduction, Structure, Functional Behavior Assessment, Contingency-Based Self-Management and Self-Monitoring of Attention.   Should include Cruickshank's program recommendations about stimuli and structure. Must include necessity of FBA. (pp. 280-286)

4.   Answers should include eating problems, weight loss, others abusing medication (siblings) medication is not the total answer to ADHD, negative publicity, side effects. (pp. 286-288)

Chapter 10: Educational Approaches

Chapter Outline

49. What Conceptual Models and Education Approaches have Been Described?
    1. Medical Model
        1. Focus on cause and often little direction for practice
        2. "New medical model"- Pediatric medicine significant addition to educational programming.
    2. Diagnostic-Remedial Model
        1. Standardized Testing (compares students to other students)-programming to address deficits
        2. Remains important and controversial
        3. Implications for Teachers: test scores can be inaccurate thus may not be evaluation for instruction
    3. Behavioral Model
        1. Applied Behavioral Analysis: emphasis on empirical verification of outcomes and task analysis
        2. Direct Instruction: (DI- purchasable programs) set of instructional practices
            1. Controlling the details of instruction (use of script)
            2. Teaching component skills
            3. Teaching students to solve problems on their own (generalization)
        3. Implications for Teachers: best available evidence supports this model
    4. Cognitive Model
        1. Emphasizes specific functions
        2. Information Processing
            1. Mnemonics
        3. Metacognition or Executive Process
        4. Cognitive-behavior modification
            1. Mentalism
        5. Instruction in Mnemonics
            1. Anchored Instruction to Real Life
        6. Implications for Teachers: practices not in conflict with other models
    5. Constructivist Model
        1. Direct opposition to behaviorism model
        2. Authentic Tasks and Experiences
        3. Emphasis on intrinsic goals for learners
        4. Socially Mediated Learning
        5. Implications for Teachers: mixed research support

50. Why is it Important for Teachers to Know What Research Says about Effective Practice?
    1. No justification for using a practice unless supported by evidence
    2. Research Syntheses: Met-Analysis and Effect Size
    3. Cautions about Research Syntheses

51. How are Educational Approaches Different, and How Are They Similar?
1. How Approaches Differ
    1. Specific versus General Emphases
    2. Bottom-up versus Top-down Programming
    3. More Structured versus Less Structured Teaching
    4. Effectiveness versus Ineffectiveness
2. How Approaches are Similar
    1. Direct Assessment of Student Learning
    2. Teaching Students How to Use Strategies
    3. Extensive Opportunities to Practice

Chapter 10: Educational Approaches

True or False

1.   Conceptual models are theories derived from associated educational approaches, as a way of determining why educators teach in a certain manner.

2.   Standardized testing can reveal problems in underlying processes, which can be used to remediate academic skill deficits thus improving student achievement.

3.   Ignoring the behavioral model is very risky for teachers simply because the best available evidence supports the procedures this conceptual model employs.

4.   An essential component of constructivism is the acceptance of the behavioral parts to whole teaching model.

5.   Modality styles instruction produces more substantial benefits for students, according to research, than mnemonic (memory) strategic instruction..

Short Answer

6.   The behavioral approach assumes academic and social behaviors are learned from

    _____   _____.

7.   Cognitive Behavior Modification includes a strong emphasis on inner language.

    Therefore, teachers must use the student's _____ _____

    to guide _____.

8.   The constructivist approach believes students oversees acquire needed strategies from

    _____ and _____ _____.

9.   The behavioral approach is built on _____ _____ programming, as

    opposed to the constructivist model which emphasizes _____ _____ .

10.   The conceptual models presented are similar in three ways. They incorporate (1)

_, (2) _____ _____, and (3)

_____ _____.

Multiple Choice

11.   Task analysis means:
       A. empirical measurement of performance.
       B. detailing the sequential components to complete a task.
       C. procedures examining reinforcement.
       D. understanding social negotiation.

12.   Direct Instruction programs:
       A. refer to a teacher lecturing.
       B. use large groups of students.
       C. incorporate extensive teacher feedback.
       D. are student centered.

13.   Overall, Direct Instruction methods have:
       A. consistently demonstrated substantial benefits in academic learning.
       B. not demonstrated consistent benefits in academic learning.
       C. demonstrated mixed benefits in terms of academic learning
       D. provided fertile ground for further research in task analysis research.

14.   Which of the following statements is true?
       A. Student-centered instruction is a research validated practice.
       B. Given authentic instruction, students are capable of discovering fundamental principles
            on their own.
       C. There is no justification for using a practice that is simply preferred over a practice
            supported by empirical evidence.
       D. Teachers should consider rejecting empirical research in favor of alternative views.

15.   Which teaching method is *not* validated by research?
       A. perceptual-motor training.
       B. formative evaluation.
       C. reading comprehension instruction.
       D. academic behavior modification.

Essay

1.   Describe ABA and why it has become an important teaching tool for classrooms with
      students who are learning disabled.

2. Apply "Task Analysis" to the task of "turning in a homework assignment". From the moment the teacher gives the assignment to the student until the moment the student hands the completed assignment in to the teacher the next day.

3. Describe the Metacognition or Executive Processes you as a student use to study this textbook and remember the information contained within. Explain how you could teach this ability to a student who does not possess this ability and what conceptual model would you use and why?

4. Explain why it is important for teachers to know what research says about teaching methods? How research can be used to tell us the effectiveness of methods? And what are at least 2 of the most effective methods that are listed and described in this chapter?

5. Contrast the behavioral and constructivist models in terms of programming and teaching.

Chapter 10: Educational Approaches

Answers To Questions

1. True (p. 295)
2. False (p. 299)
3. True (p. 307)
4. False (p. 310)
5. False (p. 316)
6. environmental feedback (p. 300)
7. own language, behaviors (p. 308)
8. need, social interactions (p. 318)
9. bottom up, top down (p. 318)
10. assessment, cognitive strategies, extensive practice (p. 320)
11. B (p. 301)
12. C (pp. 301-302)
13. A (p. 306)
14. C (pp. 311-314)
15. A (p. 316)

Essay Grading Guidelines

1. Describe ABA and why it has become an important teaching tool for classrooms with students who are learning disabled (pp. 300-301)
   - measures the effects of changes in tasks and consequences on how well students acquire skills
   - emphasis on measurement of student performance of outcomes
   - employs task analysis turning steps of cognitive process into overt strategy instruction

2. Answers should specify sequentially all of the component subtasks required to accomplish the task. (pp. 301, 305)

3. Answers should include information about self-direction and planning. Further examples of teaching would emphasize overt guiding of self-talk and self-awareness using the Cognitive Model. (pp. 307-308)

4. Answers should include that there is no justification to use methods that are not supported by research as validated practice and meta-analysis studies that have adequate effect sizes can communicate what methods are effective. Methods listed and described in the chapter include mnemonic instruction, direction instruction, academic behavior modification, and formative evaluation. (pp. 313-316)

5.   Explanations of top-down and bottom up models should be provided and their link to conceptual models as well as descriptions of highly organized and less structured classrooms and what this means for teachers. (pp. 317-318)

Chapter 11: Students who Experience Difficulties with Spoken Language

Chapter Outline

52. What Is Language?

53. Are Language Problems Common in Learning Disabilities?

54. What Are the Elements of Spoken Language and Characteristics of Students with Learning Disabilities in Spoken Language?
  1. Receptive Language
  2. Expressive Language
  3. Difficulties of Students with Learning Disabilities in Receptive and Expressive Language
  4. Phonology–Definition, How it Develops, and Problems
  5. Syntax–Definition, How it Develops, and Problems
  6. Morphology–Definition, How it Develops, and Problems
  7. Semantics–Definition, How it Develops, and Problems
  8. Pragmatics–Definition, How it Develops, and Problems
  9. Metalinguistic Awareness–Definition, How it Develops, and Problems

55. How Are Spoken Language Abilities Assessed?
  1. Standardized Assessments
    1. Comprehensive Standardized Assessments
    2. Specific Standardized Assessments
  2. Informal Language Assessment Methods
  3. Methods of Monitoring Progress

56. How Can Spoken Language Problems Be Addressed?
  1. General Principles and Accommodations
  2. Semantic Feature Analysis
  3. Keyword Mnemonics
  4. Teaching in Context or Conversation
  5. Phonemic Awareness
  6. Statement Repetition

Chapter 11: Students Who Experience Difficulties with Spoken Language

Chapter Questions

Matching

Match the linguistic element with its associated descriptions

_____ 1. Speed of Delivery

_____ 2. Body Language

_____ 3. Intonation

_____ 4. Analysis of Language

A. Paralinguistic
B. Metalinguistic
C. Nonlinguistic
D. Neurolinguistic

Multiple Choice

5. Select the *best response*. The following word(s) or phrase(s) describe receptive language:
    A. paying attention to the speaker.
    B. comprehension.
    C. hearing specific sounds.
    D. All of the above.

6. As defined in the book, the process of expressive language includes:
    A. facial expression.
    B. the ability to make sounds.
    C. hand gestures.
    D. None of the above.

7. The term for individuals who have trouble thinking of the correct word is:
    A. dysarthia.
    B. apraxia.
    C. dysnomia.
    D. dysgenic.

8. Select the *incorrect* statement regarding phonemes.
    A. English has 44 phonemes.
    B. A phoneme is the smallest unit of sound.
    C. Many teachers are not taught how phonemes work.
    D. Knowledge about phonemes has little relation to reading.

9. The patterns and rules that are used to put words together into a sentence is called:

A. verb.
B. phonemic awareness.
C. syntax.
D. formatting.

10. Select the *incorrect* information regarding the development of syntax.
   A. Children before three or four often use one-word utterances that represent full sentences.
   B. It is common for children ages three and four to use sentences such as "daddy gone" to mean "daddy is not here".
   C. It is quite common for children at five years of age to combine sentences and add clauses such as "I am playing a video game with your brother".
   D. Preschool aged children use single-word verbs such as "don't" or "run" to represent full thoughts or sentences.

11. Morphology means:
   A. adding letter to the beginning or ending of a word, changes the meaning of the word.
   B. how the words sound when spoken.
   C. the process of changing one visual image into another, such as a video of a cat changed into a lion.
   D. None of the above.

12. All of the following *except one* are effective principles or methods of teaching. Please select the *least effective*:
   A. Checking for understanding to promote comprehension.
   B. Give students worksheets for more practice because practice increases success.
   C. Use modeling to demonstrate language.
   D. Use language as an intrinsic motivator.
   E. Use self-talk and parallel-talk to describe what the teacher and others are doing and thinking as the task or assignment is worked upon.

13. Select the test(s) that has (have) *nothing to do* with assessment of language.
   A. The Mbungu Ebonics Clinical Assessment (MECA, 1999)
   B. IQ tests such as the WISC-III (Wechsler, 1991)
   C. Specific assessments such as the Comprehensive Receptive & Expressive Vocabulary Test (Wallace & Hammill, 2002)
   D. Curriculum-Based Assessments (CBA)

14.   Select the *least effective* method from the following list of methods to increase English language proficiency efficiently and effectively for students with reading difficulty.
        A.   Use visual organizers to help students see what makes meanings of words unique.
        B.   Daily read-alone time of 20 minutes.
        C.   Use of keyword mnemonics to link existing knowledge with unknown concepts or vocabulary using sound and visual cues to retrieve the information.
        D.   Teaching in context to help students self-correct when an error is made.
        E.   Phonemic awareness interactions and drills with the teacher.
        F.   Repetition of statements through teacher-student or class interaction.

15.   Select the *least effective* instructional practice for English language learners as identified by Gersten and Baker (2000).
        A.   Use cooperative learning and peer tutoring methods often.
        B.   Switch back and forth between cognitive and language demands.
        C.   Use visuals to reinforce concepts and vocabulary.
        D.   Allow students to use their native language whenever they wish.
        E.   Vocabulary needs to be the curricular anchor.

Essay

1.   Describe how you would conduct Informal Language Assessments with a 1st grade student and a 7th grade student. Make sure you include the following information:
            Your strategy for gathering the information for both age groups.
            Age-appropriate sample questions for each student.
            List of physical prompts if any.

2.   What arguments and points of issue would you make to a teacher who believes students using assistive technology of any kind is "cheating" or creating an unfair advantage over students with no learning disability? Be sure to address the issue of "fairness" vs. "tools for success" in your answer.

3.   What tools or suggestions can you give parents and guardians to help their children with language deficits? Please be specific in your suggestions and list of parent/guardian help.

4.   Why is the teaching of phonemes so important when addressing student language deficits? Please be specific in your rationale and list of reasons.

5.   What are the goals of education, as you perceive them? What technology should students be allowed to use in order to achieve those goals? Be sure to include *why* you think these technologies should be allowed (rationale).

Chapter 11: Students Who Experience Difficulties with Spoken Language

Answers To Questions

1. A (pp. 325-326)
2. C (pp. 325-326)
3. A (pp. 325-326)
4. B (pp. 325-326)
5. D (p. 329)
6. B (p. 329)
7. C (p. 329)
8. D (p. 330)
9. C (p. 332)
10. C (pp. 332-333)
11. A (p. 334)
12. B (pp. 349-350)
13. A (pp. 341-347)
14. B (pp. 349-356) Note: Even though daily reading may be important to include in reading instruction, it is not an efficient method for increasing English proficiency.
15. D (p. 351)

Essay Grading Guidelines

1. Answers should include an overall strategy for making the assessment and give four or more examples of questions and physical prompts that are age appropriate, and would be more likely to achieve the desired response upon which the assessment is made. (pp. 344-347)

2. The student should include rationale regarding the concept of "tools for success" and will exhibit that he or she understands the issue and is able to articulate their position with precision and conviction. (pp. 347-348)

3. Answers should give many ideas for improving vocabulary, phonemic awareness, and comprehension through the use of word games, puzzles, asking questions, and 'read-alouds' to the child. (pp. 347-331) Note: Even though this chapter does not explicitly give ideas for interventions for parents or guardians to use, your students should be able to start generalizing classroom techniques that would be appropriate for home use to increase vocabulary and phonemic awareness, particularly from previous chapters. (pp. 109-136)

4.   Answers should include most or all of the following (or additional reasons that are legitimate and rational): helps achieve higher-ordered thinking skills; syllable identification; sound production; influences future reading speed and ability, helps to sound out new words. The answer may include a caution against focusing too much on phonics instruction for older students (p. 355; 330-355)

5.   Answers may vary since the student is asked to provide his or her own goals of education. The student will list several technologies that are relevant to the achievement of his or her stated educational goals with rationale to support. The answers between students may be quite different since they may tie the use of specific technologies to the severity of disability. (pp. 347-348; 161-163)

Chapter 12: Students who Experience Difficulties with Reading

Chapter Outline

57.   What is Reading?

58.   What Are the Major Elements of Reading?

59.   What Problems Do Students with Learning Disabilities Have in Reading?
1.   Problems with Phonology
2.   Problems with Decoding
3.   Problems with Fluency
4.   Problems with Comprehension
    1.   Syntax
    2.   Semantics
    3.   World Knowledge
    4.   Gist Comprehension

60.   How is Reading Performance Assessed?
1.   Screening
2.   Diagnosing Problems and Planning Instruction
    1.   Diagnostic Testing
    2.   Informal Reading Inventories
    3.   Clinical Teaching
3.   Monitoring Student Progress
    1.   Reading Program Assessments
    2.   Curriculum-Based Measurement
    3.   Overview of Assessment Methods

61.   How Common Are Reading Problems in Learning Disabilities?

62.   How Can Instruction Help Prevent Reading Disabilities?
1.   Teaching Phonemic Awareness
2.   Teaching Phonics
    1.   Miscellaneous Phonics
    2.   Analytic Phonics
    3.   Synthetic Phonics
3.   Teaching Other Aspects of Early Reading
4.   Putting it All Together

63. How Can Instruction Help Remediate Learning Disabilities in Reading?
    1. Historical Approaches
        1. Fernald Approach
        2. Hegge-Kirk-Kirk Approach
        3. Orton-Gillingham Approach
    2. Contemporary Approaches
        1. Reading Recovery
        2. Corrective Reading Program
        3. Computer-Assisted Instruction
    3. Instructional Tactics
        1. Fluency Enhancement
        2. Peer-Mediated Instruction
        3. Reciprocal Teaching
        4. Comprehension Strategies

Chapter 12: Students Who Experience Difficulties with Reading

Chapter Questions

True or False

1. Predicting the outcome of a story can be an effective strategy to help students with reading difficulty.

2. Allowing students to explore how to use story maps on their own while the teacher grades papers, is an efficient use of time in the classroom.

3. One-sentence summarizing and paragraph shrinking are two methods of teaching summarizing.

4. Model-lead-test is an effective method for teaching beginning phonics.

5. Peer-mediated instruction occurs when one student provides instruction for another student.

Multiple Choice

6. Select the *best* response. Reading is:
   A. most effective when the "Matthew Effect" is operating.
   B. the most common difficulty experienced by students with learning disabilities.
   C. not related to a students' self-worth.
   D. best described by theorists.

7. Select the best response. What skill(s) is/are needed to sound out simple words?
   A. directionality in reading.
   B. sound-symbol relationships.
   C. blending.
   D. Automaticity.
   E. All of the above.

8. Select the correct statement.
   A. Because reading is closely related to spoken language, lack of phonological awareness will impact reading ability.
   B. Reversals are currently considered an excellent indicator of learning disabilities.
   C. Dyslexia is caused by the mother having taken cocaine or alcohol during pregnancy.
   D. Segmenting and blending of phonemes is not necessary when reading silently.

9.   Select the *incorrect* statement regarding comprehension.
      A.   Difficulties with reading comprehension can often be attributed to poor decoding skills.
      B.   According to LaBerge & Samuels (1973), readers have a limited supply of "units of mental attention" and having to focus on decoding leaves less units for comprehension.
      C.   The number of words students can read aloud correctly in a minute is arbitrary and has limited usefulness in helping teachers evaluate student reading problems.
      D.   Students who read at delayed levels will experience problems in comprehension.

10.   Which statement is correct regarding the alphabetic principle?
      A.   It is not as important as some researchers claim.
      B.   The teaching of phonics and the alphabetic principle by direct instruction is more effective than other instruction techniques.
      C.   Children with reading difficulties should be encouraged to discover for themselves how to convert print into spoken language equivalents; this helps them create meaning for themselves.
      D.   All children should memorize and be able to recite the alphabetic principle.

11.   According to the 1997 National Reading Panel, which method is the *most effective* in phonics instruction?
      A.   miscellaneous phonics.
      B.   synthetic phonics.
      C.   descriptive phonics.
      D.   analytic phonics.

12.   Select the *best* answer.
      A.   Fernald (1943) is the name most readily associated with multisensory approaches to the teaching of reading.
      B.   Hegge, Kirk and Kirk (1970) emphasize the use of multiple modalities during reading instruction.
      C.   Gillingham and Stilman (1965) teach students to learn associations between letters and their sounds using visual, auditory, and kinesthetic approaches.
      D.   In addition to historical methods, teachers also use programs such as Reading Recovery (Clay, 1985), Corrective Reading (Englemann et al., 1999), and Computer Assisted Instruction.
      E.   All of the above.

13.   Class Wide Peer Tutoring *does not include* the following component:
      A.   weekly competition.
      B.   a highly structured tutoring experience.
      C.   all pupil performance is kept private due to legal concerns.
      D.   direct practice.

14. Select the *incorrect* statement regarding comprehension strategies.
    A. Use of strategies such as sequence questions, helps students determine what was 1st, 2nd, or 3rd in a story or passage.
    B. The Gist comprehension training by Williams, Brown, Silverstein and deLani (1994) helps all students gain greater ability in identifying themes and main ideas of passages.
    C. Teachers give students the comprehensive passage to read and allow them the freedom necessary to discover the main idea.
    D. Story grammar involves asking questions about the important aspects of a written passage such as "Who was involved?" and "What happened?".

15. Select the *best* statement regarding story mapping.
    A. Story mapping is a visual organizer used to teach structural elements of a story.
    B. Story mapping helps students anticipate and look for key information as they read.
    C. The goal of story mapping is to have students internalize key features of stories.
    D. All of the above are correct.

Essay

1. When you encounter students that have difficulty with reading and need your help, does it matter if they are identified LD or not? If the child is merely "at-risk", do they need to be identified and labeled LD before you provide services? Why?

2. What is your plan to increase vocabulary for all your students? Does your plan include methods proven to be effective for all students? Do you have "fall-back" plans for when things do not turn out as expected? Explain.

3. Provide a simple explanation of Bloom's Taxonomy describing at least 4 of the 6 levels of cognition. What can you do specifically to help your students move their thinking and "brain power" to the higher levels?

4. When your district or school budget does not allow you the financial means to purchase needed resources, what can you do? Politically, you can only go so far and still keep your job. Are there things you can do outside the "system" to get those resources? Explain your plan.

5. Is your effectiveness as a teacher measured by the success or non-success of your students learning to read? What outside factors (to the school) make your job more difficult? Is there anything you can do to minimize those external factors?

Chapter 12: Students Who Experience Difficulties with Reading

Answers To Questions

1. True (p. 402)
2. False (pp. 403-404)
3. True (pp. 398-399)
4. True (p. 405)
5. True (p. 397)
6. B (pp. 361-362)
7. E (p. 366)
8. A (p. 367-369)
9. C (pp. 370-372)
10. B (pp. 383-385)
11. B (p. 387)
12. E (p. 389)
13. C (p. 397)
14. C (pp. 398-400)
15. D (pp. 403-404)

Essay Grading Guidelines

1. The main objective of this question is to find out if your students are actually thinking about how special education services are to be provided. Chapter 12 seems to imply that all or most of reading remediation occurs in the general education classroom. This is probably the case for most students with LD. Therefore, are your students generalizing and pulling together from various parts of the book, a defendable argument for their beliefs as well as the reality of providing services in the general education classroom (see the CEC Knowledge Check at the bottom of p. 382). Answers could actually be of two different types. 1) There may be a rationale given from the perspective of administration; that is, teachers should not give services unless or until students are identified. This may include the concept of where the services are provided such as "resource room" and "pull-out" services and may also talk about funding issues of special education. 2) There may be another rationale given from the perspective of an educator in an ideal setting. This may include the argument that teachers have been hired to educate students whether they are identified or not, with an ethical argument that all students deserve the chance to excel and succeed. The argument that these kinds of services may be provided in an inclusive or collaborative setting may also be given. (pp.104-106; 388-399)

2. Most likely your students will be providing special education services in the general education classroom and need to start internalizing their own concrete strategies for helping *all* students. Answers should include sections on assessment such as informal assessment and/or CBA, as well as more formal assessments. Look for rationale as to why a particular assessment strategy is included in their plan. The answer should also include at least one "fall-back" plan or tactic for increasing vocabulary and why that was chosen or believed to be useful. (pp. 375-381; 382; 389-400)

3. Answers should identify five of the following six cognitive levels: Knowledge, Comprehension, Application, Analysis, Synthesis, Evaluation. Answers will be varied, but look for specific and creative ways that your students list that will challenge all students, including those with special needs. (pp.375; 388)

4. Answers should include the dynamics of relationships between teachers, administrators, parents/guardians, and outside resources. The simple answer is to just use informal assessment and CBA. Look for creativity in the answers such as: communicate your assessment need to a nearby university, college, or professional testing center. Trade testing materials or testing services with other schools, districts, or schools in other states. Use the internet to network with others in need of similar services to find out what they may have done. There may be other creative answers as well. (pp. 375-381)

5. While answers will vary, your students should begin to feel some responsibility for student reading outcomes. Your students also need to balance that responsibility with the reality of the situation. Your students will not be able to solve *every* problem nor reach *every* student. Answers that only point to the external factors and do not address the issue of individual teacher responsibility to the student, are not complete answers. Answers should also list or suggest how to slow or minimize those external factors through parent/guardian education and involvement in the education process. (pp. 382-385; 393)

Chapter 13: Students who Experience Difficulties with Writing

Chapter Outline

64. What Handwriting Problems Do Students Experience?
    1. Problems with Letter Formation
        1. Far-Point and Near-Point Copying
        2. Reversal Errors
    2. Problems with Fluency
    3. Causes and Effects of Handwriting Problems

65. How is Handwriting Performance Assessed?
    1. Planning Handwriting Instruction
    2. Monitoring Handwriting Progress
        1. Curriculum-Based Assessment

66. What Interventions Can Help with Handwriting Difficulties?
    1. Teacher Modeling and Student Practice
    2. Reinforcement
    3. Self-Instruction Training

67. What Spelling Problems Do Students Experience?
    1. Spelling Errors
        1. Phoneme
        2. Grapheme
        3. Orthography
    2. Effects of Spelling Problems
        1. Phonemic Awareness, Decoding and Encoding

68. How is Spelling Performance Assessed?
    1. Standardized Assessment
    2. Planning Spelling Instruction
        1. Error Analysis
        2. Informal Spelling Inventories
    3. Monitoring Progress in Spelling

69. What Interventions Help Students' Spelling Difficulties?
    1. Developmental Interventions
        1. Morphograph
        2. Scaffolding
    2. Remedial Interventions

3. Effective Teaching Procedures
   1. Test-Study-Test
   2. Practice Procedures
   3. Time Delay
   4. Morphographic Spelling
   5. Add-a-word

70. What Composition Problems Do Students Experience?

71. How is Composition Performance Assessed?
    1. Screening
    2. Planning Composition Instruction
    3. Monitoring Progress in Composition

72. What Interventions Help Students with Composition Difficulties?
    1. Developmental Interventions
    2. Remedial Interventions
    3. Effective Teaching Procedures
       1. Self-Regulated Strategy Development
       2. Learning Strategy Interventions
       3. Explicit Teaching of the Steps in the Writing Process
       4. Explicit Teaching of the Conventions of a Writing Genre
       5. Guided Feedback
       6. Reinforcement
       7. Story Grammar
       8. Cognitive-Behavioral Techniques

Chapter 13: Students Who Experience Difficulties with Writing

Chapter Questions

Matching

_____ 1.   Written language disorder that concerns   A. Orthography
           mechanical writing skills   B. Error Analysis
                                                        C. Scaffolding
_____ 2.   Formal name for representing spoken   D. Dysgraphia
           language in a written form   E. Phonemic Awareness

_____ 3.   Ability to manipulate the smallest units
           in spoken words

_____ 4.   Informal method of teacher assessment
           that involves teacher noting certain
           types of mistakes a student makes when
           doing academic work

_____ 5.   Instructional technique in which the
           teacher provides assistance as the
           student is first learning a task, but
           gradually removes help so that the
           student can do the task
           independently

True or False

6.   Students who have handwriting problems usually do not have problems with fluency.

7.   Using Curriculum-Based Assessment to evaluate both legibility and speed of handwriting is an effective and useful tool that can be used daily in many subject areas.

8.   Informal Spelling Inventories are not a good method by which to test students as they use words from readings and class work.

9.   Using progressive time delay is a very effective technique for teachers to obtain the correct answer to a question asked.

10. Spelling is not an area that incorporates progress monitoring.

Multiple Choice

11.   Out of the nine characteristics commonly exhibited by students with dysgraphia, which of the following is *not* one of the characteristics?
       A.   Letters that are too large, too small, or inconsistent in size.
       B.   Consistent slant of cursive letters.
       C.   Incorrect use of capital and lower case letters.
       D.   Slow writing even when asked to write as quickly as possible.

12.   Select the *incorrect* component of effective handwriting instruction:
       A.   teaching of letter names.
       B.   teacher modeling.
       C.   listening to words on tape.
       D.   copying quickly to improve writing fluency.

13.   Spelling performance *cannot* be assessed in which of the following?
       A.   standardized assessment.
       B.   error analysis.
       C.   guess and check method.
       D.   Informal Spelling Inventories.

14.   There are several interventions that help students with spelling difficulties, which of the following is *most* effective?
       A.   presenting words in sentences or paragraphs.
       B.   have students make up their own study methods to coincide with their own "mental map".
       C.   using test-study-test method.
       D.   memorize the spelling list.

15.   Students with learning disabilities manifested in handwriting are *more likely* to have problems in which other area(s)?
       A.   reading and spelling.
       B.   math and science.
       C.   physical education.
       D.   social skills.

Essay

1.   Explain which interventions can help students with composition difficulties.

2.   List four of the five techniques used in teaching spelling to students with learning disabilities and give examples of each.

3.   What are some problems associated with assessing writing? What assessment techniques

can be used?

4.   What does exemplary writing instruction in the classroom look like? What kinds of activities are happening?

5.   Explain some of the most common difficulties experienced by students with learning disabilities in regards to composition writing.

Chapter 13: Students Who Experience Difficulties with Writing

Answers to Questions

1. D (p. 408)
2. A (p. 415)
3. E (p. 418)
4. B (p. 421)
5. C (p. 424)
6. False (pp. 408-409)
7. True (p. 411)
8. False (p. 426)
9. True (p. 426)
10. False (p. 420)
11. B (p. 408)
12. C (p. 413)
13. C (pp. 418-421)
14. C (p. 422)
15. A (pp. 427-430)

Essay Grading Guidelines

1. Answers could include: development interventions, echo books (Sealey, Sealey, and Millmore), remedial interventions including coordinating special education curriculum with general education curriculum, effective teaching processes such as self regulated strategy development, learning strategy interventions, explicit teaching of steps in writing process, explicit teaching of conventions of writing genre, guided feedback, reinforcements, story grammar, or cognitive behavioral techniques. (pp. 433-444)

2. Answers should include: test-study-test, practice procedures, time delay, morphographic spelling, and add a word (flow lists). Examples may include: a few spelling words each day, distributed practice, self-correction, and structured peer tutoring. (pp. 422-427)

3. Answers should include the following concepts: many students other than those with LD write poorly, many assessments only measure mechanical or editorial skills. Assessments used include: screening (tests of written language), planning composition instruction (picture story language test and TOWL), monitoring progress in composition (student samples frequently collected and scored to a standard model). (pp. 430-432)

4.   Your students should be aware of these specific features of exemplary writing instruction. They will want to emulate these in their own instructional practice. Answers should include: daily writing, prominately displayed student work, teacher-student conferences to discuss work, teacher modeling, group and individual sharing, plus others from the list on p. 435.

5.   Answers should include several of the following: planning, basic writing skills, revising, vocabulary, thematic maturity, word usage, style, sentence complexity, paragraph organization, incorporation of important elements into writing. (pp. 427-430)

Chapter 14: Students who Experience Difficulties with Mathematics

Chapter Outline

73. How Does Mathematical Knowledge Develop Normally?
1. Number sense
2. Number line
3. Whole numbers comprised of parts
4. Manipulatives
5. Sequence of development
6. Place value

74. What Problems in Mathematics Do Students Experience?
1. Problems in Cognitive Development
2. Problems in Arithmetic Performance
     1. Performance on Basic Arithmetic Tests
     2. Difficulties with Story Problems

75. How are Mathematics Abilities Assessed?
1. Achievement Tests
2. Formal Diagnostic Testing
3. Informal Inventories
4. Error Analysis
5. Monitoring Progress

76. What Interventions Help Students with Mathematics Difficulties?
1. Developmental Interventions
     1. Developmental Programs
     2. Basal Programs
2. Remedial Interventions
3. Technology
     1. Calculators
     2. Computer-Assisted Instruction
4. Effective Teaching Procedures
     1. Modeling
     2. Reinforcement
     3. Strategy Training
     4. Self-Instruction Training

Chapter 14: Students Who Experience Difficulties with Mathematics

Chapter Questions

Matching

_____ 1. Fluidity and flexibility with numbers: an understanding of what numbers mean

_____ 2. Procedure of breaking down an academic task into its component parts for instructional purposes

_____ 3. Tests used to determine which areas a student is having difficulties

_____ 4. Program used for teaching beginners fundamental math concepts

_____ 5. Severe or complete inability to perform mathematical calculations

A. Basal Programs
B. Dyscalculia
C. Diagnostic Tests
D. Number Sense
E. Task analysis

True or False

6. Out of all students, about 6 to 7% have problems learning arithmetic skills.

7. Students with learning disabilities do better on math tests that are timed.

8. Achievement tests, diagnostic tests, informal inventories, error analysis, and monitoring of progress; are all methods used to assess mathematical abilities.

9. Developmental interventions are an excellent way to introduce mathematical concepts in an exploratory or discovery style teaching methods.

10. Manipulatives are an excellent tool to teach place value to students with math difficulties.

Fill in the blank

11. Students have a concept of _____ if they understand that lengths of objects do not change when they are moved or that the amount of liquid does not change when poured into a different sized glass.

12. It is important for teachers to _____ _____ according to the curricular materials the students are using and the teacher is teaching.

13. Computers can provide the _____ and repetition that many students with learning disabilities need to master basic facts.

14. When teaching math to students with disabilities, teachers can use the following

     methods: _____, _____,

     _____ _____,

     _____-_____ _____ to help ensure
     success.

15. There is continued debate about the use of _____ in the classrooms.

16. Normally developing children learn many arithmetic operations and mathematical

     concepts before reaching school age, this is called _____

     _____.

17. Students who struggle in math try to approach story problems in a _____

     fashion rather than attempting to _____ the problem.

18. Using _____ _____ is an excellent method to note the
     particular kinds of errors a student is making when doing academic work.

19. Some students with learning disabilities have problems in both

_____and _____.

20.   Cognitive research on mathematical difficulties reveals that students with deficits in

        _____ _____ make more mistakes in giving simple
                                              answers in various areas of arithmetic.

Essay

1.   Describe the role that games play in the development of mathematic skills in preschool
        children. Since we know that mathematic skills are influenced in large part by the
        environment, and new knowledge can only 'hook' to old knowledge, what general plan
        could you describe that would help pre-school or 1ˢᵗ grade students with math difficulties.

2.   Describe if or when it would be appropriate to have a timed math test. Give a reason for
        your answer. For your students with math difficulties that also have difficulty with
        reading, describe how will you give a math test.

3.   What are the similarities and differences between Error Analysis and Monitoring
        Progress?

4.   Describe how you use or plan to use the Peer-Assisted Learning Strategy (PALS) in your
        classroom.

5.   Of all the methods described to help students with math difficulties, which two do you
        think are the most effective? Why? Is it possible to use these two methods together at the
        same time? Describe what the use of your two methods would look like in your classroom.

Chapter 14: Students Who Experience Difficulties with Mathematics

Answers to Questions

51. D (p. 453)
52. B (p. 457)
53. C (pp. 463-464)
54. A (p. 473)
55. E (p. 480)
56. True (p. 457)
57. False (p. 457)
58. True (pp. 460-470)
59. True (pp. 473-474)
60. True (p. 455)
61. conservation (p. 452)
62. monitor progress (pp. 469-470)
63. practice (pp. 476-478)
64. modeling, reinforcement, strategy training, self-instruction training (pp. 478-483)
65. calculators (p. 475)
66. informal knowledge (pp. 452-453)
67. mechanical, understanding (pp. 457-458)
68. error analysis (pp. 465-469)
69. reading, math (pp. 457-459)
70. fact retrieval (pp. 458-459)

Essay Grading Guidelines

71. Answers may include any of the following or related items concerning play and organizing: number rhymes, counting games, table games with dice or spinners, using money to count, arranging like items into separate piles, separating out dissimilar items from a pile of similar items, categorizing items by color, size, shape, or other characteristics, reading stories or poetry with numbers. The answer for the general strategy of helping pre-school or 1st grade students may include the concept of 'number sense', number line, and whole numbers comprised of parts such as 1 and 5, 2 and 4, 3 and 3 all equal the same number 6. Manipulatives may also be part of the answer. The concepts of subtraction, decimal, and place value would rarely be taught at the pre-school or 1st grade level, particularly for student with math difficulties. These last three concepts, as well as higher math skills would not be part of this answer. (pp. 452-456)

72.	Comparing the results from a timed math test and a non-timed math text, might help you discover if your students with math difficulties have a reading problem or a cognitive problem. Of course the information gathered from students reading and writing classes, as well as any previous assessment or student records, will also help to make this determination. The math test should assess the precise concepts that have been taught; problems should be aligned properly; the student should not be asked to copy problems from the board or overhead; if story problems are used students must be taught how to work them; some students may need to have the test read to them; teach students how to use a calculator and allow them to use it in the test, particularly for a student with an IEP that stipulates the use of a calculator. (p. 457; 460-470)

73.	In Error Analysis, the teacher is looking at the incorrect responses and analyzing them for incorrect facts, operations, execution of procedures. The mistakes may be random as a combination of incorrect facts or employed operations. There are also diagnostic instruments available to help in this analysis. When monitoring student progress, the teacher uses daily assignments and quizzes to learn how well the students are learning the current material. This assessment is much quicker in analysis and is specific to the curriculum concepts that need more practice. (pp. 465-470)

74.	The answers will vary depending on how effective the PALS system appears to your students. (p. 472)

75.	The answers will vary. Should include 2 methods to help students with math difficulties with explanations of why they are effective. Clear reasons why and how two could be combined and used at the same time. Description would give clear picture of understanding of how it would look and work in the classroom. (p. 483)

Chapter 15: Participation in General Education Classrooms for Students with Learning Disabilities

Chapter Outline

77. What Are the Legal Mandates for Placement?
    1. General Education Curriculum
    2. Least Restrictive Environment
    3. Continuum of Alternative Placements
    4. Regular Education Initiative
    5. Full inclusion

   B. No Child Left Behind Act
      1. Accommodations
      2. Alternative Assessments

II. How Do Students with Learning Disabilities Receive Special Education Services in General Education Classroom?
   A. Co-teaching
      1. Collaborative Consultation
   B. Resource Rooms

III. How Can Placement and Instructional Decisions Be Made?
   A. Assessing the Instructional Ecology
      1. Ecobehavioral Assessment Systems Software
      2. Informal Checklists
   B. Monitoring Student Progress
      1. Curriculum-Based Assessment
      2. Curriculum-Based Measurement

IV. What are Modifications for Students With Learning Disabilities in General Education Classrooms?
   A. Modifications Defined
      1. Adaptations
   B. Instructional Accommodations
      1. Tiered Assignments

V. What Are Effective Instructional Practices for Students with Learning Disabilities in General Education Classrooms?
   A. A Few Notes before We Begin
   B. Synthesis of Instructional Interventions
      1. Sequencing
      2. Drill-Repetition and Practice-Review

           3.   Segmentation

           4.   Directed Questioning and Responses

           5.   Controlling Difficulty of Processing Demands of a Task

           6.   Technology

           7.   Modeling of Problem-Solving Steps by the Teacher

           8.   Group Instruction

           9.   Supplements to Teacher and Peer Involvement

           10.   Strategy Cues

  C.   Graphic Organizers

           1.   Graphic Organizers

           2.   Unit Organizer

           3.   Concept Diagram

  D.   Peer-Mediated Instruction

           1.   Peer-Assisted Learning Strategies (PALS)

           2.   Collaborative Strategic Reading

           3.   Classwide Peer Tutoring

  E.   Note-Taking

  F.   General Recommendations for Science Instruction

           1.   Activities-Based Learning

           2.   Teacher Modeling

           3.   Structured Coaching

  G.   General Recommendations for Social Studies Instruction

           1.   Anchor

Chapter 15: Participation in General Education Classrooms for Students with Learning Disabilities

Chapter Questions

Matching

_____ 1.   When a teacher makes an change to instruction or assessment

_____ 2.   Special educator acts as an expert to the general educator, who is primarily responsible for instruction of students with disabilities

_____ 3.   Aids that provide students with visual representations of both concepts and facts

_____ 4.   Students with disabilities are placed in their neighborhood schools in general education classrooms for the entire day

_____ 5.   Use of peers in structured activities to provide increased opportunities for student practice with content material

A. Graphic Organizer
B. Full Inclusion
C. Peer-mediated instruction
D. Modification
E. Collaborative Consultation

True or False

1.   The No Child Left Behind Act requires that all students with disabilities do not participate in assessments of yearly progress.

2.   Supporters of co-teaching say that the technique makes an effective use of specific and unique skills of each professional to the classroom.

3.   It is important for teachers to assess the Instructional Ecology in regards to what the relationship is between the teacher and student and the instructional environment.

4.   When accommodations or modifications occur, it is important that the content of instruction is not changed.

5.   Students with learning disabilities should not be directly questioned and provided feedback because they are not engaged.

Multiple Choice

11.   Which of the following is *not* an effective instructional practice for students with learning disabilities?
      A.   segmentation.
      B.   sequencing.
      C.   immediate answer
      D.   graphic organizer.

12.   Graphic organizers are effective because they require teachers to:
      A.   describe how the components are related to the unit and to each other.
      B.   decide on how best to visually display the relationships.
      C.   identify the critical components of a unit, concept, or topic.
      D.   All of the above.

13.   Before an IEP team can make a placement and instructional decision what is *not* a consideration?
      A.   classroom data information about environment.
      B.   teacher expectations.
      C.   teacher behavior.
      D.   how long teacher has been teaching.

14.   Within the continuum of alternative placements, which of the following are *not* an options for placement?
      A.   instruction in general classroom.
      B.   special classes in hallway.
      C.   special schools.
      D.   home instruction.

15.   Which of the following is an example of graphic organizers?
      A.   outline of class notes
      B.   discussions of class running on a computer .
      C.   Concept Diagram.
      D.   multiplication chart.

Essay

1. Explain why the use of graphic organizers are successful in all content areas taught in school. Why are they so beneficial for students with learning disabilities?

2. By the time students are entering upper elementary they need to be learning note taking, what are some techniques that teachers should use? Should students with learning disabilities learn how to take notes? Explain.

3. Explain how students with learning disabilities receive special education services in the general education classroom. Give several examples.

4. Explain the differences between Curriculum-Based Assessment and Curriculum Based Measurement and how each is used with regards to students with learning disabilities.

5. On IEP's there is a place for adaptations and modifications, explain the differences of each and why each is important for students with learning disabilities.

Chapter 15: Participation in General Education Classrooms for Students with Learning Disabilities

Answers To Questions

76. D (pp. 502-507)
77. E (pp. 492-496)
78. A (pp. 511-514)
79. B (pp. 490-492)
80. C (pp. 514-515)
81. False (p. 491)
82. True (p. 493)
83. True (p. 496)
84. True (p. 505)
85. False (p. 509)
86. C (pp. 507-517)
87. D (pp. 511-514)
88. D (pp. 496-498)
89. B (p. 491)
90. C (pp. 511-514)

Essay Grading Guidelines

1. Answers should include work from Content Enhancement Routine. How does it help teachers and students. Examples from readings, graphic organizers in book and concept diagrams. (pp. 511-514)

2. Answers should include bad examples of adaptations (such as: teacher just gives the student with LD another student's notes). Document Boyles work. Chunking, outlining, guided notes, strategies, mnemonics, strategies. (pp. 516-521)

3. Include co-teaching and the philosophy behind it, collaborative consultation, models of co-teaching according to Vaughn, Schumm, Arguelles, plus resource room. (pp. 492-496)

4. Answers should include clear explanation of CBA and CBM and how each is used. Explain how the use of CBM has been shown to increase student achievement. (pp. 498-502)

5. Answers should explain differences between modifications and accommodations. Examples should include instructional adaptation and tiered assignments. (pp. 503–507)

Chapter #1 Portfolio Rubric Personal Philosophy Paper: Initial Draft

Ranking → Criteria ↓	Target	Acceptable	Unacceptable
Historical theories and major contributors	Provides a thorough description and explanation of the historical theories and its major contributors in the field of learning disabilities	Provides a description and some explanation of the historical theories and its major contributors in the field of learning disabilities	Provides an incomplete description of the historical theories and its major contributors in the field of learning disabilities
Federal laws in the field of learning disabilities	Provides a careful description of relevant federal laws applicable to the field of learning disabilities	Provides a description of relevant federal laws applicable to the field of learning disabilities	Provides an incomplete description of relevant federal laws applicable to the field of learning disabilities
Interaction of historical theories with the development of learning disabilities definitions	Explains appropriately and in full detail the relationship of historical theories with the dynamic development of learning disabilities definitions over time	Partially explains the relationship of historical theories with the dynamic development of learning disabilities definitions over time, but lacks in some details	Fails to provide a complete explanation of the relationship of historical theories with the dynamic development of learning disabilities definitions over time
Impact of definitions upon legal, ethical, and education policies and procedures	Demonstrates insightful knowledge of the impact of learning disabilities definitions upon legal, ethical and education policies and procedures	Demonstrates emerging knowledge of the impact of learning disabilities definitions upon legal, ethical and education policies and procedures	Demonstrates limited knowledge of the impact of learning disabilities definitions upon legal, ethical and education polices and procedures
Issues of definitions in relation to personal society, family, culture and label bias	Clearly identifies and describes the issues of definition relative to personal society, family, culture and label bias	Describes the issues of definition relative to personal society, family, culture and label bias	Provides an incomplete description of the issues of definition relative to personal society, family culture and label bias
Understanding of the heterogeneity of label characteristics in terms of development and lifelong effects	Shows comprehensive understanding of the heterogeneity of label characteristics in terms of development and lifelong effects	Portrays acceptable understanding of the heterogeneity of label characteristics in terms of development and lifelong effects	Shows a lack of understanding regarding heterogeneity of label characteristics in terms of development and lifelong effects
Respect toward the heterogeneity of label characteristics in terms of development and lifelong effects	Describes 2 or more examples experienced or examples noticed in others regarding respect toward the heterogeneity of label characteristics in terms of development and lifelong effects	Describes at least 1 example experienced or example noticed in others regarding respect toward the heterogeneity of label characteristics in terms of development and lifelong effects	Gives no personal example experienced or example noticed in others regarding respect toward the heterogeneity of label characteristics in terms of development and lifelong effects

Chapter #2 Portfolio Rubric Personal Philosophy Paper: Revised Draft

Ranking → Criteria ↓	Target	Acceptable	Unacceptable
Historical, philosophical, and neurological contributions vs. behavioral/environmental contributions	Provides a clear and organized description of the historical, philosophical, and neurological contributions vs. behavioral and environmental contributions to learning disability theory	Provides a complete description of the historical, philosophical, and neurological contributions vs. behavioral and environmental contributions to learning disability theory	Provides a poor and incomplete description of the historical, philosophical, and neurological contributions vs. behavioral and environmental contributions to learning disability theory
Description of the three major perspectives and its contributors	Provides a comprehensive, detailed, and organized description of the three major perspectives as well as specifics regarding each of the contributors to learning disability theory with a clear and logical link to personal philosophy	Provides a complete description of the three major perspectives as well as each of the contributors to learning disability theory with a minimal link to personal philosophy	Provides a poor and incomplete description of the three major perspectives as well as each of the contributors to learning disability theory with weak or no link to personal philosophy
Personal philosophical position on the issue of nature vs. nurture	Develops an insightful, logical, and comprehensive personal philosophical position on the issue of nature vs. nurture	Is able to determine and develop his/her own personal philosophical position on the issue of nature vs. nurture	Personal philosophical position on the issue of nature vs. nurture lacks comprehensive, logical, and clear content
Personal beliefs about the importance of understanding potential learning disability etiology and relationships to subsequent professional interaction	Cleary presents his/her beliefs on the importance of understanding potential learning disability etiology and relationships to subsequent professional interaction with students and families	Presents his/her beliefs on the importance of understanding potential learning disability etiology and relationships to subsequent professional interaction with students and families	Provides an inadequate presentation on his/her beliefs about the importance of understanding potential learning disability etiology and relationships to subsequent professional interaction with students and families
Description of how definitions and identification procedures may occur in the future due to technology and research advancement	Offers a systematically description of how definitions and identification procedures may occur in the future due to technology and research advancement	Offers an adequate description of how definitions and identification procedures may occur in the future due to technology and research advancement	Offers an unsatisfactory description of how definitions and identification procedures may occur in the future due to technology and research advancement

Chapter #3 Portfolio Rubric Action/Decision Flowchart: Information Dissemination Tool

Ranking ⟶ / Criteria ↓	Target	Acceptable	Unacceptable
Identification of the student at the top and center of the paper	Clearly identifies/describes a student who is exhibiting difficulties in a specific area(s) in the general education classroom	Identifies by characteristics a student who is exhibiting difficulties in a specific area(s) in the general education classroom	Poorly identifies a student who is exhibiting difficulties in a specific area(s) in the general education classroom
Design of two decision tracks or flowcharts from the student down each side of the paper (right and left)	Neatly designs two flowcharts which completely in detail demonstrate all the steps in the LD identification process according to the two plans: IDEA and response-to-treatment	Designs two flowcharts which demonstrate the major/required steps in the LD identification process according to the two plans: IDEA and response-to-treatment	Poorly designs two flowcharts which do not clearly demonstrate all the required steps in the LD identification process determined by the two plans: IDEA and response-to-treatment
Use of sidebars of timelines, roles, responsibilities, advantages/disadvantages, pitfalls and assessment/programmatic suggestions	Makes well and extensive use of sidebars for timelines, roles, responsibilities, advantages/disadvantages, pitfalls and assessment/programmatic suggestions	Makes limited but appropriate use of sidebars for timelines, roles, responsibilities, advantages/disadvantages, pitfalls, and assessment/programmatic suggestions	Fails to make enough use of sidebars for explanation of timelines, roles, responsibilities, advantages/disadvantages, pitfalls, and assessment/programmatic suggestions
Use of colors and shapes to highlight patterns or positive/negative points	Uses of colors and shapes enhances the understanding and illustrates the connections between various factors	Uses of colors and shapes helps to understand connections but is not clear in all cases	Use of color and shapes (of not used) is sporadic, disconnected and does not reflect the connections between concepts
Use of one sheet of paper to construct the flowchart.	Is able to fit the flowchart on one sheet of paper in order to use as an educational training tool	Flowchart major concepts fit on one sheet of paper in order to use as an educational training tool with extra information organized on an extra page	No attempt is indicated to edit the flowchart to make it fit in one sheet of paper in terms of priority content or consideration of future usage as an educational training tool
Influence of evolving laws and policies upon assessment planning and implementation	Shows complete understanding of the evolving laws/policies and influence upon assessment planning and implementation	Shows adequate understanding of the evolving laws/policies and influence upon assessment planning and implementation	Demonstrates inadequate understanding of the evolving laws/policies and influence upon assessment planning and implementation
Functions of school systems in the structure of special education	Details the organizational functions of schools systems in the structure of special education delivery	Identifies some organizational functions of schools systems in the structure of special education delivery	Lacks identification of organizational functions of schools systems in the structure of special education delivery
Describe how knowledge of the functions of school systems in the structure of special education influences the student's philosophies of special education	Demonstrates in a comprehensible manner how knowledge of the functions of schools systems in the structure of special education influences his/her philosophies of special education	Demonstrates in a clear manner how knowledge of the functions of school systems in the structure of special education influences his/her philosophies in special education	Uses poor reasoning/logic when describing how knowledge of the functions of school systems in the structure of special education influences his/her philosophies in special education

Continuation	Target	Acceptable	Unacceptable
Description of how student assessment results are used to promote positive learning results, adapt/modify learning environments, and incorporate appropriate learning technologies, taking into consideration general and special education curricula and cultural/linguistic factors	Is able to clearly define and explain how student assessment results are used to promote positive learning results, adapt/modify learning environments and incorporate appropriate learning technologies, while taking into full consideration general and special education curricula and cultural factors	Is able to give a reasonable explanation of how student assessment results are used to promote positive learning results, adapt/modify learning environments and incorporate appropriate learning technologies, while taking into consideration general and special education curricula and cultural factors	Is unable to clearly demonstrate an understanding how student assessment results are used to promote positive learning results, adapt and modify learning environments, and incorporate appropriate learning technologies. In addition, does not take into consideration general and special education curricula and/or cultural factors
Description of the ethical principles of measurement and assessment related to screening, referral, eligibility, program planning, instruction and placement for individuals with learning disabilities	Shows broad knowledge of the ethical principles of measurement and assessment related to screening referral, eligibility, program planning, instruction and placement for individuals with disabilities	Shows accurate knowledge of the ethical principles of measurement and assessment related to screening referral, eligibility, program planning, instruction and placement for individuals with disabilities	Lacks necessary knowledge of the ethical principles of measurement and assessment related to screening referral, eligibility, program planning, instruction and placement for individuals with disabilities

Portfolio Building Activity Directions:

•Begin with a "student" who is exhibiting academic, information processing, and/or social/emotional difficulties in the general education classroom at the top of your paper in the center. Describe this student briefly by specific characteristics (i.e., organizational concern, reading skill deficits, social skill problems).

•Design two decision tracks down the side of your paper from the student. These are Flowcharts, one on the right and one on the left. One Flowchart or decision track should represent the steps in the LD identification process as it exits in current IDEA law. The other Flowchart or decision track will represent the steps in - the LD identification as projected in the response to treatment reauthorized IDEA plan

•Move the Flowcharts on both tracks from the student first with identified needs to the final stages of classroom service implementation

•Include sidebars of timelines, roles, responsibilities, advantages/disadvantages, pitfalls, and assessment/programmatic suggestions

•Use colors and shapes to highlight patterns or positive/negative points

•Construct the Flowchart on 1 sheet of paper in order to use as an educational training tool when you become a special education teacher

•Remember you are attempting to depict an accurate and comprehensive representation of federal law requirements; however, portions will be influenced by your perspectives on various issues

Chapter #4 Portfolio Rubric Personal Philosophy Paper: Final Copy

Ranking → Criteria	Target	Acceptable	Unacceptable
Definition of effective models and strategies of collaboration that foster respectful and beneficial communication based on cultural perspectives and environmental characteristics and effects	Thoroughly defines what he/she believes to be effective models and strategies of collaboration that will foster respectful and beneficial communication given cultural perspectives and environmental characteristics and effects	Adequately defines what he/she believes to be effective models/strategies of collaboration that will foster respectful and beneficial communication given cultural perspectives and environmental characteristics and effects	Only partially defines what he/she believes to be effective models and strategies of collaboration that will foster respectful and beneficial communication given cultural perspectives and environmental characteristics and effects
Identification of roles and responsibilities of educators and families in the assessment and educational planning process that supports a non-biased environment and maintains a system of confidential information	Clearly and effectively identifies the roles and responsibilities of educators and families in the assessment and educational planning process that supports a non-biased environment and maintains a system of confidential information	Accurately but in a limited manner, identifies the roles and responsibilities of educators and families in the assessment and educational planning process that supports a non-biased environment and maintains a system of confidential information	Is unable to clearly and/or accurately identify the roles and responsibilities of educators and families in the assessment and educational planning process that supports a non-biased environment and maintains a system of confidential information
Discussion of how to effectively communicate, in a culturally responsive manner, with families and individuals, active participants in the planning process, while at the same time examining characteristics of your personal culture that may affect biases	Provides a comprehensive and thoughtful discussion of the techniques needed in effective culturally responsive communication, with active participatory families and individuals in the educational planning process, in addition to an insightful reflective examination of the characteristics in one's own culture that may affect biases in communication	Provides a complete discussion of the techniques needed in effective culturally responsive communication, with active participatory families and individuals in the educational planning process, in addition to a reflective examination of the characteristics in one's own culture that may affect biases in communication	Fails to provide a complete and/or thoughtful discussion of the techniques needed in effective culturally responsive communication, with active participatory families and individuals in the educational planning process, nor a reflective examination of the characteristics in one's own culture that may affect biases in communication

Chapter #4 Portfolio Rubric Personal Philosophy Paper: Final Copy

Continuation	Target	Acceptable	Unacceptable
Description of the special educator's ethical responsibility to encourage self-advocacy and independence for individuals with learning disabilities, as well as the provision of information that will link to the appropriate support services throughout their life-span	Methodically describes the special educator's ethical responsibility to encourage self-advocacy, independence, and access to appropriate life-span support services information for individuals with learning disabilities and their families	Adequately describes the special educator's ethical responsibility to encourage self-advocacy, independence, and access to appropriate life-span support services information for individuals with learning disabilities and their families	In a limited manner, describes the special educator's ethical responsibility to encourage self-advocacy, independence, and access to appropriate life-span support services information for individuals with learning disabilities and their families

Chapter #5 Semantic Map: Issues of Cultural Diversity as Related to a Learning Disability

Ranking ➝ Criteria ↓	Target	Acceptable	Unacceptable
Places "African American pre-school/early elementary student with a learning disability" in the center of the sheet	Successfully places a brief description of an "African American pre-school/early elementary student with a learning disability" in the center of the sheet	Successfully places an entry of "African American pre-school/early elementary student with a learning disability" in the center of the sheet, but an accurate student description is not provided	Fails to place the entry "African American pre-school/early elementary student with a learning disability" in the center of the sheet and/or no student description is provided
Links three boxes, which consist of needs, cultural issues, and educational issues, to the center box	Neatly links three boxes, that contain substantial information about the *needs, cultural issues and educational issues* of this "African American pre-school/early elementary student with a learning disability", to the center of the map	Links three boxes, that contain necessary but limited information about the *needs, cultural issues and educational issues* of this "African American pre-school/early elementary student with a learning disability", to the center of the map	Fails to link three boxes, that contain accurate information about the *needs, cultural issues and educational issues* of this "African American pre-school/early elementary student with a learning disability", to the center of the map
Understanding of how primary language, culture and familial background interacts with an individual's exceptional condition to impact academic and social options	Map links, connected to previous three boxes, demonstrate full comprehension of how primary language, culture and familial background interact with an individual's exceptional condition to impact academic and social options	Map links, connected to previous three boxes, demonstrates an adequate understanding of how primary language, culture and familial background interact with an individual's exceptional condition to impact academic and social options	Map links, connected to previous three boxes, demonstrates poor grasp of how primary language, culture and familial background interact with an individual's exceptional condition to impact academic and social options
Identification of instructional strategies that promote positive learning results and enhance the learning of problem-solving, self-advocacy, and self-independence for young children	Clearly and effectively identifies instructional strategies that promote positive learning results and enhance the learning of problem-solving, self-advocacy, and self-independence for young children and appropriately linking this information via creative thinking into the semantic map	Identifies instructional strategies that promote positive learning results and enhance the learning of problem-solving, self-advocacy, and self-independence for young children and appropriately linking this information into the semantic map	Unable to clearly or effectively identify instructional strategies that promote positive learning results and enhance the learning of problem-solving, self-advocacy, and self-independence for young children as well as inadequate linking of any meaningful information into the semantic map

Chapter #5 Semantic Map: Issues of Cultural Diversity as Related to a Learning Disability

Continuation	Target	Acceptable	Unacceptable
Recognition of what is needed to actively create learning environments for individuals with learning disabilities that foster cultural understanding and positive social interactions where diversity is valued	Insert map links that demonstrate thoughtful understanding by the addition of consequential map links, demonstrating what is needed to actively create learning environments for individuals with learning disabilities that foster cultural understanding and positive social interactions where diversity is valued	Insert map links that demonstrate understanding by the addition of essential map links, demonstrating what is needed to actively create learning environments for individuals with learning disabilities that foster cultural understanding and positive social interactions where diversity is valued	Does not fully recognize nor demonstrate by the addition of acceptable map links, what is needed to actively create learning environments for individuals with learning disabilities that foster cultural understanding and positive social interactions where diversity is valued
Demonstration of commitment, by special educators, to understand the culture and language, which interact with exceptionalities and to be sensitive to the many aspects of diversity, of individuals and their families	Shows broad and extensive understanding of how special educators can demonstrate a commitment to understanding the culture and language, which can interact with exceptionalities and be sensitive to the many aspects of diversity, of individuals and their families via the inclusion of accurate and various interactive connective map links	Shows satisfactory understanding of how special educators can demonstrate a commitment to understanding the culture and language, which can interact with exceptionalities and be sensitive to the many aspects of diversity, of individuals and their families via the inclusion of accurate connective map links	Shows lack of understanding of how special educators can demonstrate a commitment to understanding the culture and language, which can interact with exceptionalities and be sensitive to the many aspects of diversity, of individuals and their families with limited and/or inaccurate map links
Identification of reasons why it is vital for special educators to understand collaboration when working with families in culturally responsive ways for young children who are at risk of being labeled learning disabled	Systematically identifies reasons, linking this information expansively into the map, why it is vital for special educators to understand collaboration when working with families in culturally responsive ways for young children who are at risk of being labeled learning disabled	Adequately identifies reasons, linking this information appropriately into the map, why it is vital for special educators to understand collaboration when working with families in culturally responsive ways for young children who are at risk of being labeled learning disabled	Ineffectively identifies reasons, without linking this information correctly and/or in a limited manner into the map, why it is vital for special educators to understand collaboration when working with families in culturally responsive ways for young children who are at risk of being labeled learning disabled

Portfolio Building Activity Directions:

•Begin with a "student" who is (a) African American (b) pre-school or early elementary with a (c) learning disability. Place a center node with these three identification characteristics in the center of your paper

•Follow this with 3 linking boxes that connect to the center node. These should have headings of "Needs", "Cultural Issues", and "Educational Needs"

•From there, continue building you Semantic Map according to the information you have learned in Chapter 5 using the Evaluation Rubric as a prompt or check sheet

•For example, you may want to consider linking boxes containing information about "primary prevention" and "success for all"

•You may also find that linkages can occur across the boxes not just in linear fashion from one box to another

•Use colors, shapes, lines, and arrows to highlight patterns and specific points

•Make sure each box contains critical information and each link is clearly reasonable

•Include as much information as you have learned and can logically explain from your reading of Chapter 5

•Sometimes it helps to create brainstorm lists prior to the creation of your Semantic Map

•Attempt to create your Map on 1 sheet of paper in order to (1) use this as a conversation tool when you interview for employment or promotion and (2) use as an educational training tool in your career

•See the Companion Website for an example of a Semantic Map

Chapter #6 Transition Assessment Plan: Individualized for Shannon

Criteria / Ranking →	Target	Acceptable	Unacceptable
Development of an appropriate Transition Assessment Plan (TAP) for Shannon that contains all the components needing to be addressed in Shannon's Individualized Transition Plan (ITP)	Develops a comprehensive and appropriate Transition Assessment Plan, listing all the components necessary for Shannon's ITP according to her needs	Develops an appropriate Transition Assessment Plan, listing most of the components necessary for Shannon's ITP according to her needs	Fails to develop an appropriate Transition Assessment Plan, lists some but not all of the components needing to be addressed in Shannon's ITP according to her needs
Understanding of how, from the TAP through ITP implementation, individuals with exceptionalities, families and personnel from other appropriate agencies and related services need to be included	Identifies a comprehensive listing of the required individuals who must attend and participate in the TAP for Shannon through ITP implementation and another appropriate yet insightful suggested listing of potential individuals from additional agencies or service providers who should be considered invitees with rationales provided	Identifies a listing of the required individuals who must attend and participate in the TAP for Shannon through ITP implementation but may not include all the potential individuals from additional agencies or service providers who should be considered invitees with rationales provided	Does not identify a complete listing of the required individuals who must attend and participate in the TAP for Shannon through ITP implementation no potential related personnel
Identification of multiple types of assessments, formal and informal, as part of TAP, that will be needed to provide useful information in designing an Individualized Transition Plan for Shannon (this fits within the components previously developed)	Logically and effectively identifies multiple types of assessments, formal and informal, that will be needed to provide useful information in designing an Individualized Transition Plan which are clearly based on all of Shannon's relevant provided information and the TAP components previously developed	Identifies multiple types of assessments, formal and informal, that will be needed to provide useful information in designing an Individualized Transition Plan which are based on Shannon's given information and the TAP components previously developed	Is unable to, or in a very limited manner, identify multiple types of assessments, formal and informal, that will be needed to provide useful information in designing an Individualized Transition Plan which are based on Shannon's given information and the TAP components previously developed

Chapter #6 Transition Assessment Plan: Individualized for Shannon

Continuation	Target	Acceptable	Unacceptable
Incorporates all policies and procedures according to federal and state laws regarding the planning and assessment process of TAP	Successfully identifies and incorporates all federal and state legal policies and procedures in designing a TAP for Shannon	Identifies and incorporates most of the federal and state legal policies and procedures in designing a TAP for Shannon	Fails to clearly identify incorporates federal and state legal policies and procedures in designing a TAP for Shannon
Recognition of laws and polices, concerning the assessment and planning process of the ITP, which are specifically related to culturally responsive collaboration	Effectively and appropriately recognizes legal issues concerning the assessment and planning process of the ITP, which are specifically related to culturally responsive collaboration and includes this information in the TAP as part of valuable and legal communication facilitating advocacy and partnership	Appropriately recognizes most of the legal issues concerning the assessment and planning process of the ITP, as it relates to culturally responsive collaboration and includes this information in the TAP	Unable to recognize the legal issues concerning the assessment and planning process of the ITP, as it relates to culturally responsive collaboration and include this information in the TAP
Appropriate citations of Internet sites containing Transition Planning/Assessment Information used in the creation of Transition Assessment Plan	Includes a full list of additional active and appropriate Internet sites used in the creation of Transition Assessment Plan	Includes a limited list of additional active and appropriate Internet sites used in the creation of Transition Assessment Plan	Includes few or no additional listings of additional active Internet sites used in the creation of Transition Assessment Plan; or uses sites that are not credible academically

Chapter # 7 Proactive Behavior Management Plan: Jamal

Criteria / Ranking →	Target	Acceptable	Unacceptable
Identification of Jamal's specific behavior that needs to be changed	Clearly identifies, in measurable terms, one of Jamal's specific behaviors that needs to be changed	Adequately identifies a specific behavior of Jamal that needs to be changed	Is unable to identify in a measurable manner a specific behavior of Jamal that needs to be changed
Identification of the desired behavior that the teacher wants to use as the replacement for the unwanted behavior with Jamal	Clearly identifies, in measurable terms, an appropriate desired behavior, which can be used to replace the unwanted behavior with Jamal	Adequately identifies a specific desired behavior, which can be used to replace the unwanted behavior with Jamal	Fails to identify a specific desired and/or appropriate behavior, which can be used to replace the unwanted behavior with Jamal
Identification of the education method being used to manage the behavior problem with descriptions of specific method components	Provides an accurate description with specific component implementation details, of the current education method(s) being used to manage the Jamal's behavior problem(s)	Accurately describes the current education method(s) being used to manage Jamal's behavior problem(s)	Does not provide an accurate identification and/or description of the current education method(s) being used to manage Jamal's behavior problem(s)
Support statement agreeing or disagreeing with the teacher's method currently in use for Jamal with defense rationale	Presents a systematic discussion that demonstrates methodology support or lack thereof for Jamal with logical rationale supported by textbook information	Presents a discussion that shows whether he/she agrees or disagrees with the method the teacher is using as being the most effective one to use for Jamal and provides logical reasons for position taken	Fails to provide a complete discussion that shows whether he/she agrees or disagrees with the method the teacher is using as being the most effective one to use for Jamal or not
Selection of another behavior management method with implementation description in planning a proactive program appropriate for Jamal	Appropriately selects another behavior management method supported by research (citations) and provides a full description of the implementation steps in planning a proactive program for Jamal	Appropriately selects another behavior management method and provides a description of the implementation steps in planning a proactive program for Jamal	Behavior management method is not appropriately selected and description provides a limited and/or poor description of the implementation steps in planning a proactive program for Jamal
Defending the chosen behavior management method decided upon for Jamal	Provides comprehensive and valid arguments to support and defend his/her chosen proactive behavior management method	Provides several valid rationales to support and defend his/her chosen proactive behavior management method	Fails to provide reasons that support and defend his/her chosen behavior management method

Chapter # 7 Proactive Behavior Management Plan: Jamal

Continuation	Target	Acceptable	Unacceptable
Awareness of what needs to be done to create a learning environment for individuals with learning disabilities that fosters cultural understanding yet promotes emotional well-being, active engagement, and positive social interactions	The Proactive Behavior Management Plan for Jamal, includes techniques that demonstrate an outstanding awareness of the factors that need to be integrated into the learning environment: fostering cultural understanding, the promotion of emotional well-being, active engagement, and positive social interactions	The Proactive Behavior Management Plan for Jamal, includes at least 2 of the following 4 techniques that demonstrate awareness of the factors that need to be integrated into the learning environment: fostering cultural understanding, the promotion of emotional well-being, active engagement, and positive social interactions	The Proactive Behavior Management Plan for Jamal, includes 1 or fewer or the 4 techniques that demonstrate awareness of the factors which need to be integrated into the learning environment: fostering cultural understanding, the promotion of emotional well-being, active engagement, and positive social interactions
Recognition of the tools that educators can use to encourage student personal empowerment and independence	Incorporates at least 2 effective teaching tools, with descriptions, that can enhance personal empowerment and independence for Jamal into his Proactive Behavior Management Plan	Incorporates at least 1 effective teaching tool, with description, that can enhance personal empowerment and independence for Jamal into his Proactive Behavior Management Plan	Does not include description(s) of any effective teaching tool(s) that can enhance personal empowerment and independence for Jamal into his Proactive Behavior Management Plan
Identification of what a special educator can use for direct motivational and instructional interventions with individuals who have learning disabilities to teach them to respond effectively to current expectations	Motivational and instructional intervention examples appropriate for Jamal are built into the Proactive Behavior Management Plan so as to assist him in responding effectively to current school setting expectations	Either one motivational or one instructional intervention appropriate for Jamal is built into the Proactive Behavior Management Plan so as to assist him in responding effectively to current school setting expectations	Neither motivational nor any instructional intervention examples appropriate for Jamal are built into the Proactive Behavior Management Plan so as to assist him in responding effectively to current school setting expectations
Recognition of the importance of monitoring on a regular basis the progress of students with learning disabilities in making ongoing educational decisions	Jamal's Proactive Behavior Management Plan explains a monitoring system to assess the progress of desired behavior for the purpose of making ongoing educational decisions	Jamal's Proactive Behavior Management Plan explains a monitoring system of behavior change	Jamal's Proactive Behavior Management Plan fails to explain or selects an inappropriate monitoring system of behavior change for the purpose of making ongoing educational decisions

Chapter # 8 Information Processing: Diagram

Criteria / Ranking →	Target	Acceptable	Unacceptable
Diagram indicating movement of information as it moves from sensory register through working memory process and retrieval	Creates a comprehensive and accurate diagram which includes all possible steps through in its progress from sensory register through working memory process and retrieval	Creates an accurate diagram which includes the steps a bit of information passes through in its progress from sensory register through working memory to retrieval	Creates a diagram which includes some but not all of the essential steps a bit of information passes through in its progress from sensory register through working memory to retrieval
Knowledge such as episodic and procedural or how information is lost (displacement, decay) inserted in appropriate places	Includes extensive appropriate diagram sidebar pieces of knowledge such as episodic and procedural or how information is lost (displacement, decay) in appropriate places (how information processing conditions interact with abilities and behaviors of individuals with learning disabilities)	Includes many appropriate diagram sidebar pieces of knowledge such as episodic and procedural or how information is lost (displacement, decay) in appropriate places (how information processing conditions interact with abilities and behaviors of individuals with learning disabilities)	Includes a few or no diagram sidebar pieces of knowledge such as episodic and procedural or how information is lost (displacement, decay) in appropriate places (how information processing conditions interact with abilities and behaviors of individuals with learning disabilities)
Effects of how an individual can learn, organize, store, and retrieve information foundational to special education teaching methods in providing individualized, meaningful, and challenging instruction	Includes comprehensive sequential diagram information, in the appropriate places of memory processes, on multiple teaching methods that special education teachers can use to provide individualized, meaningful, and challenging instruction while helping students retain, organize and retrieve information	Includes diagram information, in the appropriate places of memory processes, on many teaching methods that special education teachers can use to provide individualized, meaningful, and challenging instruction while helping students retain, organize and retrieve information	Includes little or no diagram information on some teaching methods that help students retain, organize and retrieve information
Supports and adaptations that might be required for individuals with learning disabilities in order to access the general curriculum	Identifies excellent and suitable supports and adaptations that might be required for individuals with learning disabilities in order to access the general curriculum and inserts this information appropriately into the diagram	Identifies many suitable supports and adaptations that might be required for individuals with learning disabilities in order to access the general curriculum and inserts this information into the diagram	Identifies few or no appropriate supports and adaptations that might be required for individuals with learning disabilities in order to access the general curriculum

Chapter # 8 Information Processing: Diagram

Continuation	Target	Acceptable	Unacceptable
Ways in which communicating can interweave understanding of culture along with an influence on language interaction and exceptionalities with sensitivity to aspects of diversity	Thoughtfully incorporates cultural 'hot buttons' indicating ways in which communicating can interweave with aspects of diversity such as language interaction, and environmental issues	Adequately incorporates cultural 'hot buttons' indicating ways in which communicating can interweave with aspects of diversity such as language interaction, and environmental issues	Includes few or no cultural 'hot buttons' indicating ways in which communicating can interweave with aspects of diversity such as language interaction, and environmental issues

Portfolio Building Activity Directions:

•Use colors, shapes, lines, and arrows to highlight patterns and specific points

•Make sure each box contains critical information and each link is clearly reasonable

•Include as much information as you have learned and can logically explain from your reading of Chapter 8

•Sometimes it helps to create brainstorm lists prior to the creation of your Diagram

Attempt to create your Diagram on 1 sheet of paper in order to (1) share this with your students so they will [a] understand how their brains work, [b] know what they need to do in order to perform at their best, and [c] realize what they need from their teachers, so they can learn optimally, (2) use this as a conversation tool when you interview for employment or promotion and (2) use as an educational training tool in your career

Chapter # 9 Educational Recommendations with Implementations: Shannon

Ranking → / Criteria ↓	Target	Acceptable	Unacceptable
Understands how AD/HD definitional characteristics can affect an individual's behaviors and abilities to learn	Demonstrates comprehensive understanding of how AD/HD definitional characteristics affect the behaviors and abilities for an individual to learn, thus providing appropriate and realistic educational recommendations that link to Shannon's needs	Demonstrates adequate understanding of how AD/HD definitional characteristics affect the behaviors and abilities for an individual to learn, thus providing appropriate educational recommendations that link to Shannon's needs	Lacks complete understanding of how AD/HD definitional characteristics affect the behaviors and abilities for an individual to learn, thus fails to provide appropriate educational recommendations that link to Shannon's needs
Description of the evidence-based practices that will promote self-management and positive learning results for students with AD/HD and learning disabilities	Describes many research validated practices that align with Shannon's educational needs, which would promote self-management and positive learning results	Supplies several research validated practices that align with Shannon's educational needs, which would promote self-management and positive learning results	Lists few to no research validated practices that align with Shannon's educational needs, which would promote self-management and positive learning results
Ways in which the exceptionality of AD/HD can impact the roles and responsibilities of educators	Provides a detailed explanation of how each educational recommendation can be implemented thereby demonstrating comprehension of how the roles and responsibilities of educators are impacted	Provides a sufficient explanation of how each educational recommendation can be implemented thereby demonstrating knowledge of how the roles and responsibilities of educators are impacted	Provides a scarce explanation of how each educational recommendation can be implemented thereby demonstrating limited awareness of how the roles and responsibilities of educators are impacted
Understanding of how educators shape learning environments (intrinsic and extrinsic motivation) in order to encourage personal empowerment and effective responding for students with AD/HD and learning disabilities	Shannon's plan incorporates in an insightful manner extrinsic and intrinsic motivation in educational recommendations and implementations documenting clear understanding of how educators shape learning environments in order to encourage personal empowerment and effective responding	Shannon's plan incorporates extrinsic and intrinsic motivation in educational recommendations and implementations documenting understanding of how educators shape learning environments in order to encourage personal empowerment and effective responding	Shannon's plan includes few or inappropriate include extrinsic and intrinsic motivation in educational recommendations and implementations; therefore, no understanding of how educators shape learning environments in order to encourage personal empowerment and effective responding is demonstrated

Chapter # 10 Direct Instruction Lesson Plan Rubric: Create a Concept Map

Criteria → Ranking	Target	Acceptable	Unacceptable
Lesson Plan includes the sequence of all the necessary components as supported by research necessary to promote positive learning results for individuals with learning disabilities as well as indicates how it contributes to the ongoing analysis of the student's learning progress	Lesson Plan correctly incorporates 11 instructional components: a teacher-led lesson that is structured with clearly stated objective, level of accuracy expected, relevance to the student's life, application of how the student can learn the information, explicit modeling, opportunities for the student to respond, extensive guided practice/feedback, and link back to future instruction	Lesson Plan correctly incorporates 7-10 instructional components: a teacher-led lesson that is structured with clearly stated objective, level of accuracy expected, relevance to the student's life, application of how the student can learn the information, opportunities for the student to respond, extensive guided practice/feedback, and link back to future instruction	Lesson Plan correctly incorporates less than 7 instructional components: a teacher-led lesson that is structured with clearly stated objective, level of accuracy expected, relevance to the student's life, application of how the student can learn the information, opportunities for the student to respond, extensive guided practice/feedback, and link back to future instruction
Lesson Plan includes task analysis of the concept taught	Correctly and appropriately includes task analysis in the Direct Instruction Lesson Plan	Includes task analysis in the Direct Instruction Lesson Plan	Fails to include task analysis in the Direct Instruction Lesson Plan, or uses task analysis inappropriately
Lesson Plan includes scripted frequent questions as part of the assurance of mastery, fluency, and ongoing analysis of student's learning progress	Lesson Plan incorporates, according to task analysis, and lesson objective, scripted and frequent (> 15) teacher led questions which are used to ensure adequate guided practice and student mastery of the content as well as learning progress analysis as detailed in the lesson	Lesson Plan incorporates, according to task analysis, and lesson objective, scripted and average number (10-14) of teacher led questions which are used to ensure adequate guided practice and student mastery of the content as well as learning progress analysis as detailed in the lesson	Lesson Plan incorporates, according to task analysis, and lesson objective, scripted and infrequent (<9) teacher led questions which are used to ensure adequate guided practice and student mastery of the content as well as learning progress analysis as detailed in the lesson
Description of the components of Direct Instruction that research that research has indicated are necessary to promote positive learning results for individuals with learning disabilities	Provides a comprehensive description of the components of Direct Instruction that research has indicated are necessary to promote positive learning results for individuals with learning disabilities	Provides an appropriate description of the components of Direct Instruction that research has indicated are necessary to promote positive learning results for individuals with learning disabilities	Provides an incomplete description of the components of Direct Instruction that research has indicated are necessary to promote positive learning results for individuals with learning disabilities

Chapter # 11 Keyword Mnemonics Rubric: Language Instructional Intervention

Criteria / Ranking →	Target	Acceptable	Unacceptable
Knowledge of how to determine a student's language area content needs by the administration of a pretest measuring vocabulary	Administers a vocabulary pretest using a paper and pencil (stimulus and response) or paper and tape recorder (stimulus and response) and links the results directly to student knowledge of word meanings to determine instructional needs	Administers a vocabulary pretest without a student stimulus and response hard copy or does not link the results directly to student knowledge of word meanings to determine instructional needs	Administers a vocabulary pretest without a student stimulus and response hard copy and does not link the results directly to student knowledge of word meanings to determine instructional needs
Identification and use of a research-based instructional intervention, Keyword Mnemonics, that can be used to promote positive learning results in the area of language deficits	Employs results from student pretest to design and deliver student instruction using Keyword Mnemonics (a. uses 5x7 index cards for each vocabulary word, b. works with the student to include all the necessary components of the intervention on the index card, c. satisfactorily teaches the vocabulary intervention to someone from outside the class, d. uses color to assist in memory, e. uses exaggeration to assist in memory)	Employs results from student pretest to design and deliver student instruction using Keyword Mnemonics and completes 3-4 of the 5 items listed	Does not necessarily employ results from student pretest to design and deliver student instruction using Keyword Mnemonics and/or completes less than 3 of the items listed
Administration of formative and summative assessments in order to measure student vocabulary learning	Instruction includes several self-quizzing attempts of each vocabulary word using the Keyword index cards and a recording sheet (formative), this is followed by a summative paper and pencil (stimulus and response) or paper and tape recorder (stimulus and response) assessment to determine learning mastery	Instruction includes several self-quizzing attempts of each vocabulary word using the Keyword index cards (formative), this is followed by a summative paper and pencil (stimulus and response) or paper and tape recorder (stimulus and response) assessment to determine learning mastery	Instruction is followed by a hard copy summative assessment to determine learning mastery
Understanding of how special education professionals can enhance language development for individuals with cultural and linguistic differences	Summarizes the a. design, b. delivery, and c. results of instruction with specifics on the potential impact cultural diversity has on a student's ability to learn vocabulary (linguistic differences)	Summarizes adequately 2 of the following 3 a. design, b. delivery, and c. results of instruction along with some information on the potential impact cultural diversity has on a student's ability to learn vocabulary (linguistic differences)	Summary is minimal on 2 of the following 3 a. design, b. delivery, and c. results of instruction and provides little or no information on the potential impact cultural diversity has on a student's ability to learn vocabulary (linguistic differences)

Chapter # 12 Reading Summative Table: Contemporary Reading Approaches and Instructional Tactics

Criteria / Ranking →	Target	Acceptable	Unacceptable
Create a table with headings that can be used to analyze reading interventions for individuals with learning disabilities	Table is original computer generation with 6 columns (method, skills, description, strengths, concerns, research) and 9 rows (one for each method presented in the chapter), and the table has an appropriate Title related to Reading Interventions	Table may not be an original computer generation and/or it may only contain 5 of the 6 columns (method, skills, description, strengths, concerns, research) and/ or 7-8 of the 9 rows (one for each method presented in the chapter), and/or may not have an appropriate Title related to Reading Interventions	Table may not be an original computer generation and/or it may contain less than 5 of the 6 columns (method, skills, description, strengths, concerns, research) and/ or less than 7 of the 9 rows (one for each method presented in the chapter), and/or may not have an appropriate Title related to Reading Interventions
Recognition of research supported instructional interventions that will enhance reading performance skills for individuals with learning disabilities	Complete listing of research supported instructional interventions, in the methods column of the table, which special education teachers can use that will enhance reading performance skills	Lists 7-8 of the 9 research supported instructional interventions, in the methods column of the table, which special education teachers can use that will enhance reading performance skills	Lists less than 7 of the 9 research supported instructional interventions, in the methods column of the table, which special education teachers can use that will enhance reading performance skills
Definition of what reading performance skills can be developed by each research instructional intervention	Specifies, in reading performance terms (measurable objectives), the skills addressed by each of the instructional methods listed in the table	Lists the skills addressed by each of the instructional methods listed in the table	Lists general reading skills for some but not all of the instructional methods listed in the table
Description of reading interventions including areas of strengths and concerns	Detailed, comprehensive, and accurate information about each instructional method listed in the table addressing: a. generalization and maintenance across environments, b. helping general education colleagues integrate students into inclusive settings, and c. analysis of assistive technologies as being appropriate for students	Accurate information about each instructional method listed in the table addressing either 2 of the 3 items listed and/or contains some inaccurate information	Incomplete information about instructional methods listed in the table and/or addressing 2 or less of the 3 items listed across the methods
Link of instructional method to research findings	Accurate and complete listing of research findings, both positive and negative, applicable to the field of learning disabilities for each method listed	Listing of research findings, may not be complete and/or may not contain both positive and negative points, applicable to the field of learning disabilities for each method listed	Inaccurate and/or incomplete listing of research findings applicable to the field of learning disabilities for each method

Chapter # 13 Language Arts Instruction: Jamal

Criteria / Ranking ➝	Target	Acceptable	Unacceptable
Understands written language research-based interventions that can be used to improve the performance skills of students with learning disabilities	Provides a systematic explanation of 3 research supported methods Jamal's teacher is using to teach handwriting and 2 research supported methods Jamal's teacher is using to teach spelling	Provides an adequate explanation of 2 out of the 3 research supported methods Jamal's teacher is using to teach handwriting and 1 out of the 2 research supported methods Jamal's teacher is using to teach spelling	Fails to provide an adequate explanation for 2 out of the 3 research supported methods Jamal's teacher is using to teach handwriting or 1 out of the 2 research supported methods Jamal's teacher is using to teach spelling
Comprehends specific components of language research-based interventions that can be used to improve the performance skills of students with learning disabilities	Selects and describes 3 additional appropriate handwriting methods and 2 additional appropriate spelling methods which are: a. research based, b. can incorporate assistive technology, c. include meaningful self-management, and d. active engagement	Selects and describes 2 out of 3 additional appropriate handwriting methods and 1 out of 2 additional appropriate spelling methods which addresses at least 3 of the following aspects of instruction: a. research based, b. can incorporate assistive technology, c. include meaningful self-management, and d. active engagement	Selects and describes 1 out of 3 additional appropriate handwriting methods or 1 out of 2 additional appropriate spelling methods which address at least 2 of the following aspects of instruction: a. research based, b. can incorporate assistive technology, c. include meaningful self-management, and d. active engagement
Recognizes the importance specific instructional variables as supported by research for the improvement of student performance	When describing additional language research-based methods, comprehensive information is provided on teacher explicit modeling and student guided practice to assure acquisition and fluency, as well as regular progress monitoring for the purpose of improving student performance	When describing additional language research-based methods, information is provided on 2 of the following 3 items: teacher explicit modeling and student guided practice to assure acquisition and fluency, as well as regular progress monitoring for the purpose of improving student performance	When describing additional language research-based methods, information is provided on less than 2 of the following 3 items: teacher explicit modeling and student guided practice to assure acquisition and fluency, as well as regular progress monitoring for the purpose of improving student performance

Chapter # 14 Evaluation Software Programs: Math Instruction

Criteria ⟶ Ranking ⟶	Target	Acceptable	Unacceptable
Designs an evaluation tool based Box 14.5 "Today's Technology for Learning Disabilities: 10 Tips for Choosing Math Software"	Designs an evaluation tool based on Box 14.5 "Today's Technology for Learning Disabilities: 10 Tips for Choosing Math Software"	Designs an evaluation tool based on at least 7-9 items from the Box 14.5 "Today's Technology for Learning Disabilities: 10 Tips for Choosing Math Software"	Designs an evaluation tool based on less than 7 of the items from the Box 14.5 "Today's Technology for Learning Disabilities: 10 Tips for Choosing Math Software"
Include in the evaluation tool information about what current research says about effective math instruction	Include in the evaluation tool items that relate to what research says about effective math instruction: a. guided practice, b. ongoing analysis of progress, c. student independence and empowerment	Include in the evaluation tool at least 2 of the 3 items that relate to what research says about effective math instruction: a. guided practice, b. ongoing analysis of progress, c. student independence and empowerment	The evaluation tool includes only 1 of the 3 items that relate to what research says about effective math instruction: a. guided practice, b. ongoing analysis of progress, c. student independence and empowerment
Evaluate math software programs according to current evidence-based practices, resources available, and student academic needs	Comprehensively evaluates three math software programs using his/her evaluation tool as to their effectiveness and usefulness for instruction and assessment in a summative narrative	Evaluates three math programs using his/her evaluation tool but does not necessarily address the program's effectiveness and usefulness for instruction or assessment in a summative narrative	Evaluates less than three math programs using his/her evaluation tool and/or does not address the program's effectiveness and usefulness for instruction and assessment in a summative narrative

Chapter # 15 Lesson and Support Materials Design: Spelling, Reading Comprehension, or Mathematics

Criteria / Ranking →	Target	Acceptable	Unacceptable
Creates a spelling, reading, comprehension or math lesson based on research validated instructional design	Successfully designs a spelling, reading comprehension or math lesson which includes details of all the instructional steps supported by research as described for effective instruction in the chapter (i.e., explicit modeling, guided practice, and ongoing progress analysis in a collaborative context)	Successfully designs a spelling, reading comprehension or math lesson which includes with 70-80% accuracy the details of the instructional steps supported by research as described for effective instruction in the chapter (i.e., explicit modeling, guided practice, and ongoing progress analysis in a collaborative context)	Designs a spelling, reading comprehension or math lesson which includes with less than 70% accuracy the details of the instructional steps supported by research as described for effective instruction in the chapter (i.e., explicit modeling, guided practice, and ongoing progress analysis in a collaborative context)
Identification of research-based instructional interventions which can promote achievement gains in general education classrooms and curricula	Successfully identifies a research-based instructional intervention, which can promote achievement gains in general education classrooms and curricula and uses this to design a spelling, reading comprehension or math lesson	Identifies a research-based instructional intervention, which can promote achievement gains in general education classrooms and curricula but does not fully incorporate the required components of the intervention into the design of a spelling, reading comprehension or math lesson	Does not identify a research-based instructional intervention, which can promote achievement gains in general education classrooms and curricula and does not incorporate the required components of any specific intervention into the design of a spelling, reading comprehension or math lesson
Constructs materials of professional quality that she/he can later use in the classroom	Constructs a variety of original professional quality materials (8-10 documents) that support the delivery of the lesson design (i.e., teacher instruction and students curriculum)	Constructs a variety of original quality materials (5-7 documents) that support the delivery of the lesson design (i.e., teacher instruction and students curriculum)	Constructs a variety of materials (less than 5 documents) that support the delivery of the lesson design (i.e., teacher instruction and students curriculum).
Development of lesson and supporting materials demonstrates understanding of why students with learning disabilities must have individualized instruction in order to provide meaningful and challenging educational opportunities	Shows excellent understanding of why students with learning disabilities must have individualized instruction planning providing meaningful and challenging opportunities (i.e., uses performance based lesson outcomes that align with sufficient guided practice and independent practice using engaging and meaning materials, etc.)	Shows sufficient understanding of why students with learning disabilities must have individualized instruction planning providing meaningful and challenging opportunities (i.e., uses performance based lesson outcomes that align with sufficient guided practice and independent practice using engaging and meaning materials, etc.)	Shows inadequate understanding of why students with learning disabilities must have individualized instruction planning providing meaningful and challenging opportunities (i.e., uses performance based lesson outcomes that align with sufficient guided practice and independent practice using engaging and meaning materials, etc.)

Teaching Tips for First-time Instructors and Adjunct Professors

Teaching Tips Contents

1. How to be an Effective Teacher
Seven principles of good teaching practice
Tips for Thriving: Creating an Inclusive Classroom

2. Today's Undergraduate Students
Traditional students
Nontraditional students
Emerging influences
What students want from college professors
Tips for Thriving: Be a "Facilitator of Learning"

3. Planning Your Course
Constructing the syllabus
Problems to avoid
Tips for Thriving: Visual Quality

4. Your First Class
Seven goals for a successful first meeting
Tips for Thriving: An Icebreaker

5. Strategies for Teaching and Learning
Getting participation through active learning
Team learning
Tips for Thriving: Active Learning and Lecturing

6. Grading and Assessment Techniques
Philosophy of grading
Criterion grading
Tips for Thriving: Result Feedback

7. Using Technology
Advice on using the web in small steps
Tips for Thriving: Using Videos

8. Managing Problem Situations
Cheating
Unmotivated students
Credibility problems
Tips for Thriving: Discipline

9. Surviving When You're Not Prepared
Contingency plans

10. Improving Your Performance
Self evaluation
Tips for Thriving: Video-Recording Your Class

1 How to be an Effective Teacher

(Adapted from Royse, *Teaching Tips for College and University Instructors: A Practical Guide*, published by Allyn & Bacon, Boston, MA, ©2001, by Pearson Education)

A look at 50 years of research "on the way teachers teach and learners learn" reveals seven broad principles of good teaching practice (Chickering and Gamson, 1987).

1. Frequent student-faculty contact: Faculty who are concerned about their students and their progress and who are perceived to be easy to talk to, serve to motivate and keep students involved. Things you can do to apply this principle:

- ✓ Attend events sponsored by students.
- ✓ Serve as a mentor or advisor to students.
- ✓ Keep "open" or "drop-in" office hours.

2. The encouragement of cooperation among students: There is a wealth of research indicating that students benefit from the use of small group and peer learning instructional approaches. Things you can do to apply this principle:

- ✓ Have students share in class their interests and backgrounds.
- ✓ Create small groups to work on projects together.
- ✓ Encourage students to study together.

3. Active learning techniques: Students don't learn much by sitting in the classroom listening; they must talk about what they are learning, write about it, relate to it, and apply it to their lives. Things you can do to apply this principle:

- ✓ Give students actual problems or situations to analyze.
- ✓ Use role-playing, simulations or hands-on experiments.
- ✓ Encourage students to challenge ideas brought into class.

4. Prompt feedback: Learning theory research has consistently shown that the quicker the feedback, the greater the learning. Things you can do to apply this principle:

- ✓ Return quizzes and exams by the next class meeting.
- ✓ Return homework within one week.
- ✓ Provide students with detailed comments on their written papers.

5. Emphasize time on task: This principle refers to the amount of actual involvement with the material being studied and applies, obviously, to the way the instructor uses classroom instructional time. Faculty need good time-management skills. Things you can do to apply this principle:

- ✓ Require students who miss classes to make up lost work.
- ✓ Require students to rehearse before making oral presentations.
- ✓ Don't let class breaks stretch out too long.

6. Communicating high expectations: The key here is not to make the course impossibly difficult, but to have goals that can be attained as long as individual learners stretch and work hard, going beyond what they already know. Things you can do to apply this principle:

- ✓ Communicate your expectations orally and in writing at the beginning of the course.
- ✓ Explain the penalties for students who turn work in late.
- ✓ Identify excellent work by students; display exemplars if possible.

7. Respecting diverse talents and ways of learning: Within any classroom there will be students who have latent talents and some with skills and abilities far beyond any that you might imagine. Understanding your students as individuals and showing regard for their unique talents is "likely to facilitate student growth and development in every sphere – academic, social, personal, and vocational" (Sorcinelli, 1991, p.21). Things you can do to apply this principle:

- ✓ Use diverse teaching approaches.
- ✓ Allow students some choice of readings and assignments.
- ✓ Try to find out students' backgrounds and interests.

 Tips for Thriving: Creating an Inclusive Classroom

How do you model an open, accepting attitude within your classroom where students will feel it is safe to engage in give-and-take discussions? Firstly, view students as individuals instead of representatives of separate and distinct groups. Cultivate a climate that is respectful of diverse viewpoints, and don't allow ridicule, defamatory or hurtful remarks. Try to encourage everyone in the class to participate, and be alert to showing favoritism.

---

2   Today's Undergraduate Students

(Adapted from: Lyons et al, *The Adjunct Professor's Guide to Success*, published by Allyn & Bacon, Boston, MA, ©1999, by Pearson Education)

Total enrollment in all forms of higher education has increased over 65% in the last thirty years. Much of this increase was among part-time students who now comprise over 70% of total college enrollment. The number of "nontraditional" students, typically defined as 25 years of age or older, has been growing more rapidly than the number of "traditional" students, those under 25 years of age. Though there is a great deal of common ground between students of any age, there are some key differences between younger and older students.

Traditional students: Much more than in previous generations, traditional students are the products of dysfunctional families and have had a less effective primary and secondary education. Traditional students have been conditioned by the aftermath of high-profile ethical scandals (such as Watergate), creating a mindset of cynicism and lack of respect for authority figures – including college professors. Students of this generation are quick to proclaim their "rights". Many of today's students perceive professors as service providers, class attendance as a matter of individual choice, and grades as "pay" to which they are entitled for meeting standards they perceive as reasonable.

Nontraditional students: Many older students are attending college after a long lay-off, frequently doubting their ability to succeed. The other time-consuming challenges in their lives – children, work, caring for aging parents – often prevent adequate preparation for class or contribute to frequent absences. While traditional students demand their "rights," many older students won't ask for the smallest extra consideration (e.g., to turn a project in a few days late). Most older students learn best by doing, by applying the theory of the textbook to the rich set of experiences they have accumulated over the years.

Emerging influences: Today, a fourth of all undergraduate students are members of minority groups. Obviously, ethnicity, language, religion, culture, and sexual orientation are each significant issues to which a professor should be sensitive. The successful professor sees these differences as an opportunity rather than a threat to learning.

 Tips for Thriving: Be a "Facilitator of Learning"

Be energized by students who "don't get it" rather than judgmental of their shortcomings. View yourself as a "facilitator of learning" rather than a "sage on a stage."

What students want from college professors: While each student subgroup has particular characteristics that affect the dynamics of a college learning environment, students consistently need the following from their college instructors:

- ✓ Consistently communicated expectations of student performance that are reasonable in quantity and quality
- ✓ Sensitivity to the diverse demands on students and reasonable flexibility in accommodating them
- ✓ Effective use of classroom time
- ✓ A classroom environment that includes humor and spontaneity
- ✓ Examinations that address issues properly covered in class and are appropriate to the level of the majority of the students in the class
- ✓ Consistently positive treatment of individual students

The new paradigm of "colleges and universities as service providers to consumer-oriented students" is now firmly entrenched. The successful professor will do well to embrace it.

3   Planning Your Course

(Adapted from Royse, *Teaching Tips for College and University Instructors: A Practical Guide*, published by Allyn & Bacon, Boston, MA, ©2001, by Pearson Education)

Constructing the syllabus: The syllabus should clearly communicate course objectives, assignments, required readings, and grading policies. Think of the syllabus as a stand-alone document. Those students who miss the first or second meeting of a class should be able to learn most of what they need to know about the requirements of the course from reading the syllabus. Start by collecting syllabi from colleagues who have recently taught the course you will be teaching and look for common threads and themes.

Problems to avoid: One mistake commonly made by educators teaching a course for the first time is that they may have rich and intricate visions of how they want students to demonstrate comprehension and synthesis of the material, but they somehow fail to convey this information to those enrolled. Check your syllabus to make sure your expectations have been fully articulated. Be very specific. Avoid vaguely worded instructions:

Instruction	Students may interpret as:
"Write a short paper."	Write a paragraph.
	Write half a page.
	Type a two-page paper.
"Keep a log of your experiences."	Make daily entries.
	Make an entry when the spirit moves me.
	At the end of term, record what I recall.
"Obtain an article from the library."	Any magazine article.
	An article from a professional journal.
	A column from a newsletter.

 Tips for Thriving: Visual Quality

Students today are highly visual learners, so you should give special emphasis to the visual quality of the materials you provide to students. Incorporate graphics into your syllabus and other handouts. Color-code your materials so material for different sections of the course are on different colored papers. Such visuals are likely to create a perception among students that you are contemporary.

4 Your First Class

(Adapted from: Lyons et al, *The Adjunct Professor's Guide to Success*, published by Allyn & Bacon, Boston, MA, ©1999, by Pearson Education)

Success in achieving a great start is almost always directly attributable to the quality and quantity of planning that has been invested by the course professor. If the first meeting of your class is to be successful, you should strive to achieve seven distinct goals.

Create a Positive First Impression: Renowned communications consultant Roger Ailes (1996) claims you have fewer than 10 seconds to create a positive image of yourself. Students are greatly influenced by the visual component; therefore you must look the part of the professional professor. Dress as you would for a professional job interview. Greet each student entering the room. Be approachable and genuine.

Introduce Yourself Effectively: Communicate to students who you are and why you are credible as the teacher of the course. Seek to establish your approachability by "building common ground," such as stating your understanding of students' hectic lifestyles or their common preconceptions toward the subject matter.

Clarify the Goals and Expectations: Make an acetate transparency of each page of the syllabus for display on an overhead projector and using a cover sheet, expose each section as you explain it. Provide clarification and elicit questions.

Conduct an Activity that Introduces Students to Each Other: Students' chances of being able to complete a course effectively is enhanced if each comes to perceive the classmates as a "support network." The small amount of time you invest in an icebreaker will help create a positive classroom atmosphere and pay additional dividends throughout the term.

 Tips for Thriving: Icebreaker

The following activity allows students to get acquainted, exchange opinions, and consider new ideas, values or solutions to problems. It's a great way to promote self-disclosure or an active exchange of viewpoints.

Procedure

1. Give students one or more Post-it™ notes
2. Ask them to write on their note(s) one of the following:
   a. A *value* they hold
   b. An *experience* they have had recently
   c. A *creative idea* or solution to a problem you have posed
   d. A *question* they have about the subject matter of the class
   e. An *opinion* they hold about a topic of your choosing
   f. A *fact* about themselves or the subject matter of the class
3. Ask students to stick the note(s) on their clothing and circulate around the room reading each other's notes.
4. Next, have students mingle once again and negotiate a trade of Post-it™ notes with one another. The trade should be based on a desire to possess a particular value, experience, idea, question, opinion or fact for a short period of time. Set the rule that all trades have to be two-way. Encourage students to make as many trades as they like.
5. Reconvene the class and ask students to share what trades they made and why. (e.g., "I traded for a note that Sally had stating that she has traveled to Eastern Europe. I would really like to travel there because I have ancestors from Hungary and the Ukraine.")

(Adapted from: Silverman, *Active Learning: 101 Strategies to Teach Any Subject*, published by Allyn & Bacon, Boston, MA, ©1996, by Pearson Education).

Learn Students' Names: A student who is regularly addressed by name feels more valued, is invested more effectively in classroom discussion, and will approach the professor with questions and concerns.

Whet Students' Appetite for the Course Material: The textbook adopted for the course is critical to your success. Your first meeting should include a review of its approach, features, and sequencing. Explain to students what percentage of class tests will be derived from material from the textbook.

Reassure Students of the Value of the Course: At the close of your first meeting reassure students that the course will be a valuable learning experience and a wise investment of their time. Review the reasons why the course is a good investment: important and relevant content, interesting classmates, and a dynamic classroom environment.

5   Strategies for Teaching and Learning

(Adapted from: Silverman, *Active Learning: 101 Strategies to Teach Any Subject,* published by Allyn & Bacon, Boston, MA, ©1996, by Pearson Education)

Getting participation through active learning: To learn something well, it helps to hear it, see it, ask questions about it, and discuss it with others. What makes learning "active"? When learning is active, students do most of the work: they use their brains to study ideas, solve problems, and apply what they learn. Active learning is fast-paced, fun, supportive, and personally engaging. Active learning cannot occur without student participation, so there are various ways to structure discussion and obtain responses from students at any time during a class. Here are ten methods to get participation at any time:

1. **Open discussion**. Ask a question and open it up to the entire class without further structuring.
2. **Response cards**. Pass out index cards and request anonymous answers to your questions.
3. **Polling**. Design a short survey that is filled out and tallied on the spot.
4. **Subgroup discussion**. Break students into subgroups of three or more to share and record information.
5. **Learning partners**. Have students work on tasks with the student sitting next to them.
6. **Whips**. Go around the group and obtain short responses to key questions – invite students to pass if they wish.
7. **Panels**. Invite a small number of students to present their views in front of the class.
8. **Fishbowl**. Ask a portion of the class to form a discussion circle and have the remaining students form a listening circle around them. Bring new groups into the inner circle to continue the discussion.
9. **Games**. Use a fun exercise or quiz game to elicit students' ideas, knowledge, or skill.
10. **Calling on the next speaker**. Ask students to raise their hands when they want to share their views and ask the current speaker to choose the next speaker.

(Adapted from Royse, *Teaching Tips for College and University Instructors: A Practical Guide*, published by Allyn & Bacon, Boston, MA, ©2001, by Pearson Education)

Team learning: The essential features of this small group learning approach, developed originally for use in large college classrooms are (1) relatively permanent heterogeneous task groups; (2) grading based on a combination of individual performance, group performance, and peer evaluation; (3) organization of the course so that the majority of class time is spent on small group activities; (4) a six-step instructional process similar to the following model:

1. Individual study of material outside of the class is assigned.
2. Individual testing is used (multiple choice questions over homework at the beginning of class)
3. Groups discuss their answers and then are given a group test of the same items. They then get immediate feedback (answers).
4. Groups may prepare written appeals of items.

5. Feedback is given from instructor.
6. An application-oriented activity is assigned (e.g. a problem to be solved requiring input from all group members).

If you plan to use team learning in your class, inform students at the beginning of the course of your intentions to do so and explain the benefits of small group learning. Foster group cohesion by sitting groups together and letting them choose "identities" such as a team name or slogan. You will need to structure and supervise the groups and ensure that the projects build on newly acquired learning. Make the projects realistic and interesting and ensure that they are adequately structured so that each member's contribution is 25 percent. Students should be given criteria by which they can assess and evaluate the contributions of their peers on a project-by-project basis (Michaelsen, 1994).

 Tips for Thriving: Active Learning and Lecturing

Lecturing is one of the most time-honored teaching methods, but does it have a place in an active learning environment? There are times when lecturing can be effective. Think about the following when planning a lecture:

Build Interest: Capture your students' attention by leading off with an anecdote or cartoon.
Maximize Understanding and Retention: Use brief handouts and demonstrations as a visual backup to enable your students to see as well as hear.
Involve Students during the Lecture: Interrupt the lecture occasionally to challenge students to answer spot quiz questions.
Reinforce the Lecture: Give students a self-scoring review test at the end of the lecture.

---

6 Grading and Assessment Techniques

(Adapted from Wankat, *The Effective, Efficient Professor: Teaching, Scholarship and Service*, published by Allyn & Bacon, Boston, MA, ©2002, by Pearson Education)

Philosophy of grading: Develop your own philosophy of grading by picturing in your mind the performance of typical A students, B students and so on. Try different grading methods until you find one that fits your philosophy and is reasonably fair. Always look closely at students on grade borders – take into account personal factors if the group is small. Be consistent with or slightly more generous than the procedure outlined in your syllabus.

Criterion grading: Professor Philip Wankat writes: "I currently use a form of criterion grading for my sophomore and junior courses. I list the scores in the syllabus that will guarantee the students As, Bs and so forth. For example, a score of 85 to 100 guarantees an A; 75 to 85, a B; 65 to 75, a C; and 55 to 65, a D. If half the class gets above 85% they all get an A. This reduces competition and allows students to work together and help each other. The standard grade gives students something to aim for and tells them exactly what their grade is at any time. For students whose net scores are close to the borders at the end of the course, I look at other factors before deciding a final grade such as attendance."

 Tips for Thriving: Result Feedback

As stated earlier, feedback on results is the most effective of motivating factors. Anxious students are especially hungry for positive feedback. You can quickly and easily provide it by simply writing "Great job!" on the answer sheets or tests. For students who didn't perform well, a brief note such as "I'd love to talk with you at the end of class" can be especially reassuring. The key is to be proactive and maintain high standards, while requiring students to retain ownership of their success.

7 Using Technology

(Adapted from: Sanders, *Creating Learning-Centered Courses for the World Wide Web*, published by Allyn & Bacon, Boston, MA, ©2001, by Pearson Education)

The Web as a source of teaching and learning has generated a great deal of excitement and hyperbole. The Web is neither a panacea nor a demon, but it can be a valuable tool. Among the many misunderstandings about the use of Web pages for teaching and learning is a view that such efforts must encompass an entire course. Like any other tool in a course (e.g. lectures, discussions, films, or field trips) online material can be incorporated to enhance the learning experience.

The best way to start using the Web in a course is with small steps. Developing a single lesson or assignment, a syllabus, or a few well-chosen links makes more sense than trying to develop a whole course without sufficient support or experience. Testing Web materials with a class that regularly meets face-to-face helps a faculty member gauge how well a lesson using the Web works. Making adjustments within the context of a traditional class helps fine-tune Web lessons that may be offered in distance education without face-to-face interaction.

 Tips for Thriving: Using Videos

Generally a videotape should not exceed half and hour in length. Always preview a video before showing it to ensure the content, language, and complexity are appropriate for your students. Include major videos on your syllabus to encourage attendance and integrate them into the context of the course. Plan to evaluate students' retention of the concepts on exams or through reports. Avoid reinforcing the common student perception that watching a video is a time-filler.

By beginning with good practices in learning, we ask not how the new technology can help us do a better job of getting students to learn, but rather we ask how good pedagogy be better implemented with the new technology.

8 Managing Problem Situations

(Adapted from Wankat, *The Effective, Efficient Professor: Teaching, Scholarship and Service*, published by Allyn & Bacon, Boston, MA, ©2002, by Pearson Education)

Cheating: Cheating is one behavior that should not be tolerated. Tolerating cheating tends to make it worse. Prevention of cheating is much more effective than trying to cure it once it has occurred. A professor can prevent cheating by:

- Creating rapport with students
- Gaining a reputation for giving fair tests
- Giving clear instructions and guidelines before, during, and after tests
- Educating students on the ethics of plagiarism
- Requiring periodic progress reports and outlines before a paper is due

Try to develop exams that are perceived as fair and secure by students. Often, the accusation that certain questions were tricky is valid as it relates to ambiguous language and trivial material. Ask your mentor or an experienced instructor to closely review the final draft of your first few exams for these factors.

Tips for Thriving: Discipline

One effective method for dealing with some discipline problems is to ask the class for feedback (Angelo & Cross, 1993) In a one-minute quiz, ask the students, "What can I do to help you learn?" Collate the responses and present them to the class. If behavior such as excessive talking appears in some responses (e.g. "Tell people to shut up") this gives you the backing to ask students to be quiet. Use of properly channeled peer pressure is often effective in controlling undesired behavior

(Adapted from Royse, *Teaching Tips for College and University Instructors: A Practical Guide*, published by Allyn & Bacon, Boston, MA, ©2001, by Pearson Education)

Unmotivated Students: There are numerous reasons why students may not be motivated. The "required course" scenario is a likely explanation – although politics in colonial America is your life's work, it is safe to assume that not everyone will share your enthusiasm. There are also personal reasons such as a death of a loved one or depression. Whenever you detect a pattern that you assume to be due to lack of motivation (e.g. missing classes, not handing assignments in on time, non-participation in class), arrange a time to have the student meet with you outside the classroom. Candidly express your concerns and then listen.

Motivating students is part of the faculty members' job. To increase motivation professors should: show enthusiasm for the topic; use various media and methods to present material; use humor in the classroom; employ activities that encourage active learning; and give frequent, positive feedback.

(Adapted from Baiocco/Waters, *Successful College Teaching*, published by Allyn & Bacon, Boston, MA, ©1998, by Pearson Education)

Credibility Problems. If you are an inexperienced instructor you may have problems with students not taking you seriously. At the first class meeting articulate clear rules of classroom decorum and comport yourself with dignity and respect for students. Try to exude that you are in charge and are the "authority" and avoid trying to pose as the students' friend.

9   Surviving When You're Not Prepared

(Adapted from: Lyons et al, *The Adjunct Professor's Guide to Success*, published by Allyn & Bacon, Boston, MA, ©1999, by Pearson Education)

Despite your thorough course planning, your concern for students, and commitment to the institution, situations will arise – illness, family emergencies – that prevent you from being fully prepared for every class meeting. Most students will excuse one flawed performance during a term, but try to develop contingency plans you can employ on short notice. These might include:

- Recruiting a guest speaker from your circle of colleagues to deliver a presentation that might interest your students.
- Conducting a carousel brainstorming activity, in which a course issue is examined from several perspectives. Divide the students in to groups to identify facts appropriate to each perspective. For example, you might want to do a SWOT analysis (Strengths, Weaknesses, Opportunities, Threats) on a particular organization or public figure.
- Dividing the class into groups of three or four and asking them to develop several questions that would be appropriate for inclusion on your next exam.
- Identify a video at your local rental store that embellishes material from the course.
- Assign students roles (e.g. press, governmental figures, etc.), and conduct a focused analysis of a late-breaking news story related to your course.
- Divide students into groups to work on an assigned course project or upcoming exam.
- As a last resort, admit your inability to prepare a class and allow students input into formulating a strategy for best utilizing class time.

In each case, the key is to shift the initial attention away from yourself (to permit you to gather your thoughts) and onto an activity that engages students in a new and significant way.

10   Improving Your Performance

(Adapted from: Lyons et al, *The Adjunct Professor's Guide to Success*, published by Allyn & Bacon, Boston, MA, ©1999, by Pearson Education)

The instructor who regularly engages in systematic self-evaluation will unquestionably derive greater reward from the formal methods of evaluation commonly employed by colleges and universities. One method for providing structure to an ongoing system of self-evaluation is to keep a journal of reflections on your teaching experiences. Regularly invest 15 or 20 introspective minutes following each class meeting to focus especially on the strategies and events in class that you feel could be improved. Committing your thoughts and emotions enables you to develop more effective habits, build confidence in your teaching performance, and make more effective comparisons later. The following questions will help guide self-assessment:

> *How do I typically begin the class?*
> *Where/How do I position myself in the class?*
> *How do I move in the classroom?*
> *Where are my eyes usually focused?*
> *Do I facilitate students' visual processing of course material?*
> *Do I change the speed, volume, energy, and tone of my voice?*
> *How do I ask questions of students?*
> *How often, and when, do I smile or laugh in class?*
> *How do I react when students are inattentive?*
> *How do I react when students disagree or challenge what I say?*
> *How do I typically end a class?*

 Tips for Thriving: Video-Recording Your Class

In recent years a wide range if professionals have markedly improved their job performance by employing video recorders in their preparation efforts. As an instructor, an effective method might be to ask your mentor or another colleague to tape a 10 to 15 minute mini-lesson then to debrief it using the assessment questions above. Critiquing a videotaped session provides objectivity and is therefore more likely to effect change. Involving a colleague as an informal coach will enable you to gain from their experience and perspective and will reduce the chances of your engaging in self-depreciation.

References

Ailes, R. (1996) *You are the message: Getting what you want by being who you are*. New York: Doubleday.

Chickering, A.W., & Gamson, Z.F. (1987) Seven principles for good practice in undergraduate education. AAHE Bulletin, 39, 3-7.

Michaelson, L.K. (1994). Team Learning: Making a case for the small-group option. In K.W. Prichard & R.M. Sawyer (Eds.), *Handbook of college teaching*. Westport, CT: Greenwood Press.

Sorcinelli, M.D. (1991). Research findings on the seven principles. In A.W. Chickering & Z. Gamson (eds.), *Applying the seven principles of good practice in undergraduate education*. New Directions for Teaching and Learning #47. San Francisco: Jossey-Bass.